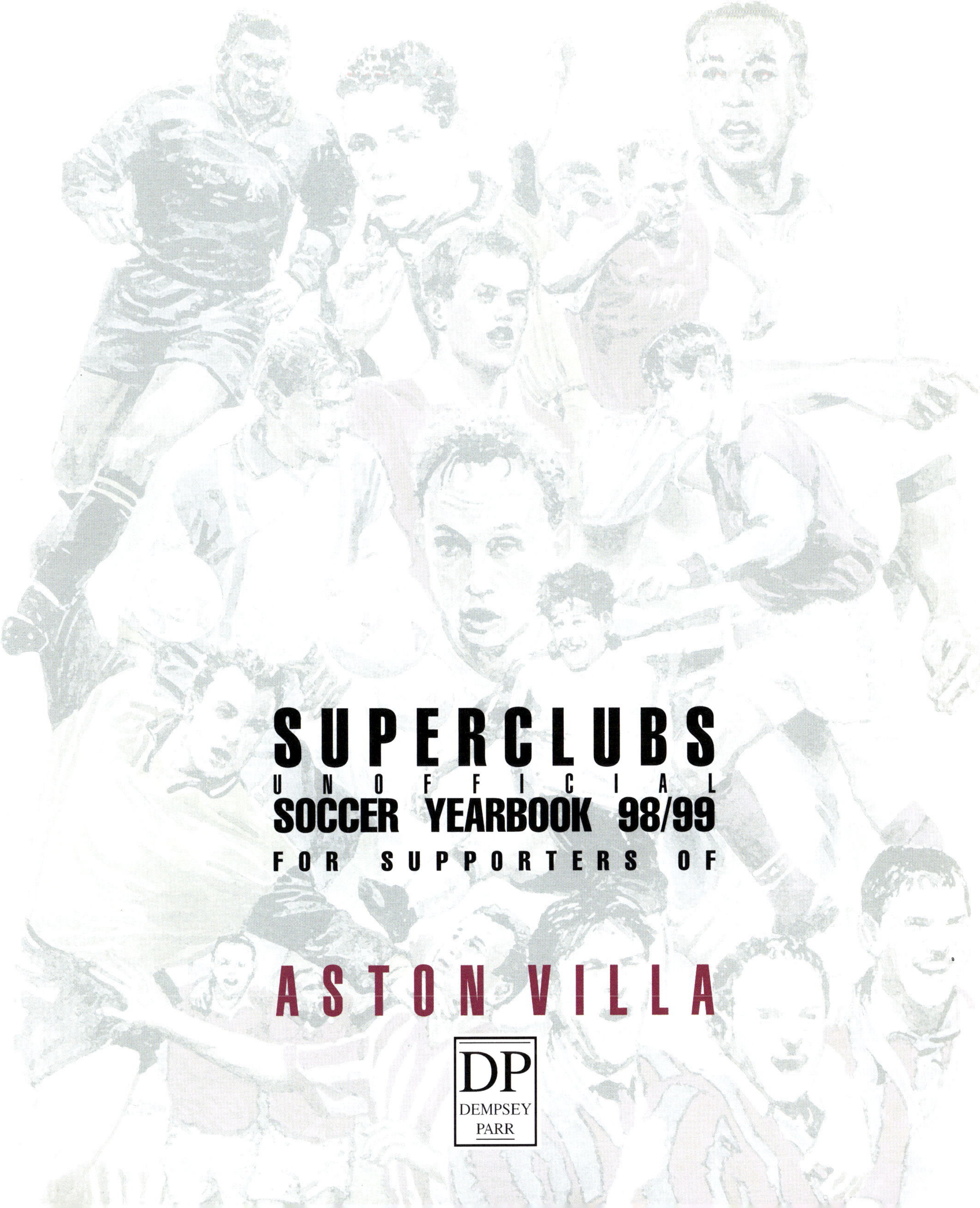

SUPERCLUBS

UNOFFICIAL

SOCCER YEARBOOK 98/99

FOR SUPPORTERS OF

ASTON VILLA

DP
DEMPSEY PARR

First published in Great Britain in 1998 by
Dempsey Parr
13 Whiteladies Road
Clifton
Bristol BS8 1PB

ISBN: 1840840625

Produced for Dempsey Parr by
Prima Creative Services

Editorial director Roger Kean
Managing editor Tim Smith (Content E.D.B.)
Contributing authors
Steve Bradley
Jim Drewett (Deadline Features)
Steve Farragher
Sam Johnstone
Alex Leith (Deadline Features)
Rex Nash
Russell Smith
Tim Smith

Cover background and illustrations by Oliver Frey

Design and repro by Prima Creative Services

Printed and bound in Italy by L.E.G.O., Vicenza

Picture Acknowledgements
The publisher would like to thank the staff of Allsport and Action Images for their unstinting help and all the other libraries, newspapers and photographers who have made this edition possible. All pictures are credited alongside the photograph.

ALLSPORT

SUPERCLUBS
UNOFFICIAL
SOCCER YEARBOOK 98/99
FOR SUPPORTERS OF

ASTON VILLA

CONTENTS

STATISTICS

One of England's most famous and illustrious clubs, Aston Villa have scored more league goals than any other club in the country. The Villans can also claim to be one of the most successful clubs in the history of the British game, having won the league and the cup on seven occasions each. Without doubt, though, Villa's greatest triumph came in 1982 when a Peter Withe goal brought the European Cup back to Birmingham for the first time.

Both main and inset: Allsport

Date Formed:	1874
Date Entered Football League:	1888
Former Names:	None
Official Nickname:	The Villans
Other Nicknames:	Villa

New boy John Gregory in pensive mood as the Villans take on Liverpool, 28/2/98

Remember this moment? Goalscorers Dwight Yorke, Savo Milosevic and Ian Taylor hoist aloft the Coca-Cola Cup after beating Leeds 3–0 in 1996

MANAGERS SINCE JOINED LEAGUE:

George Ramsay	(1884–1926)	Vic Crowe	(1970–74)
W.J. Smith	(1926–34)	Ron Saunders	(1974–82)
Jimmy McMullan	(1934–35)	Tony Barton	(1982–84)
Jimmy Hogan	(1936–44)	Graham Turner	(1984–86)
Alex Massie	(1945–50)	Billy McNeill	(1986–87)
George Martin	(1950–53)	Graham Taylor	(1987–90)
Eric Houghton	(1953–58)	Dr. Jozef Venglos	(1990–91)
Joe Mercer	(1958–64)	Ron Atkinson	(1991–94)
Dick Taylor	(1965–67)	Brian Little	(1994–98)
Tommy Cummings	(1967–68)	John Gregory	(1998–)
Tommy Docherty	(1968–70)		

CLUB HONOURS

Premier League Runners-Up
1993

Division One Champions
1894, 1896, 1897, 1899, 1900, 1910, 1981

Division One Runners-Up
1889, 1903, 1908, 1911, 1913, 1914, 1931, 1933, 1990

Division Two Champions
1938, 1960

Division Two Runners-Up
1975, 1988

Division Three Champions
1972

FA Cup Winners 1887 (April 2nd, Kennington Oval)
Aston Villa v West Bromwich Albion, 2–0
Scorers: Hodgetts, Hunter

FA Cup Winners 1895 (April 20th, Crystal Palace)
Aston Villa v West Bromwich Albion, 1–0; Scorer: Chatt

FA Cup Winners 1897 (April 10th, Crystal Palace)
Aston Villa v Everton 3–2
Scorers: Campbell, Wheldon, Crabtree

FA Cup Winners 1905 (April 15th, Crystal Palace)
Aston Villa v Newcastle United 2–0; Scorer: Hampton (2)

FA Cup Winners 1913 (April 19th, Crystal Palace)
Aston Villa v Sunderland 1–0; Scorer: Barber

FA Cup Winners 1920 (March 24th, Stamford Bridge)
Aston Villa v Huddersfield Town 1–0 (aet); Scorer: Kirton

FA Cup Winners 1957 (May 4th, Wembley)
Aston Villa v Manchester United 2–1
Scorer: McParland (2)

FA Cup Runners-Up 1892 (March 9th, Kennington Oval)
Aston Villa v West Bromwich Albion 0–3

FA Cup Runners-Up 1924 (April 27th, Wembley)
Aston Villa v Newcastle United 0–2

League Cup Winners 1961 (First Leg: August 22nd, Rotherham)
Aston Villa v Rotherham United 0–2
(Second Leg: September 5th, Villa Park)
Aston Villa v Rotherham United 3–0 (3–2 on aggregate)
Scorers: O'Neill, Burrows, McParland

League Cup Winners 1975 (March 1st, Wembley)
Aston Villa v Norwich City 1–0; Scorer: Graydon

League Cup Winners 1977 (March 12th, Wembley)
Aston Villa v Everton 0–0 (aet)

ALLSPORT

Riccardo Scimeca battles with Kiko of Atletico Madrid in the UEFA Cup quarter-final

(March 16th, Hillsborough)
Aston Villa v Everton 1– 1 (aet); Scorer: Kenyon (og)

(April 13th, Old Trafford)
Aston Villa v Everton 3–2; Scorers: Nicholl, Little (2)

League Cup Winners 1994 (March 27th, Wembley)
Aston Villa v Manchester United 3–1
Scorers: Atkinson, Saunders (2)

League Cup Winners 1996 (March 24th, Wembley)
Aston Villa v Leeds United 3–0; Scorers: Milosevic, Taylor, Yorke

European Cup Winners 1982 (May 26th, Rotterdam)
Aston Villa v Bayern Munich 1–0; Scorer: Withe

Chairman: H.D. Ellis
Club Sponsors: AST Computers

Record Attendance: 76,588 against Derby County, FA Cup 6th Round, March 2nd 1946

Stadiums: 1874–76 Aston Park
1876–97 Perry Barr
1897– Villa Park
Address: Villa Park, Trinity Road, Birmingham B6 6HE
Capacity: 39,339
Stands: Holte End, Trinity Road Stand, North Stand, Doug Ellis Stand
Prices: Adults £17, £19, £22
Children £8.50, £11; OAPs £8.50, £11
Season ticket prices: Adults £289–£374;
Concessions £144.50–£197;
Full-time students £200–£235
Parking facilities: 1,000 permit holders at the ground, 600 at Aston Villa Leisure Centre, Aston Hall Road

PITCH DIMENSIONS

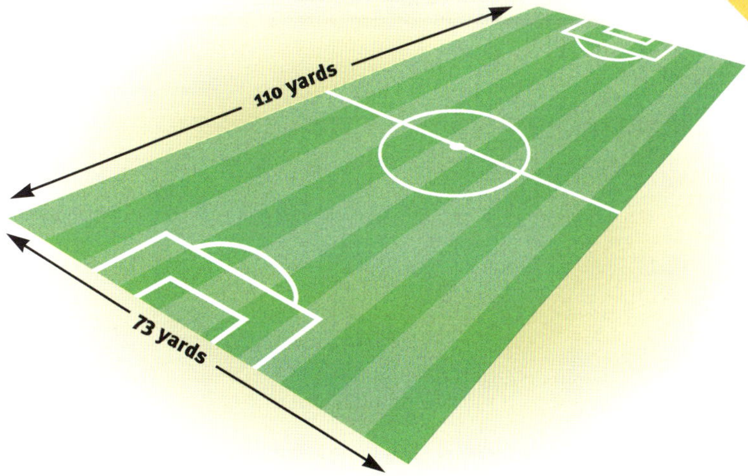

BEST PUB

The Aston Hotel, corner of Witton Lane and Witton Road – roomy pub close to the ground. Popular with home supporters, drawback membership scheme in operation. (**Heroes and Villains** fanzine)

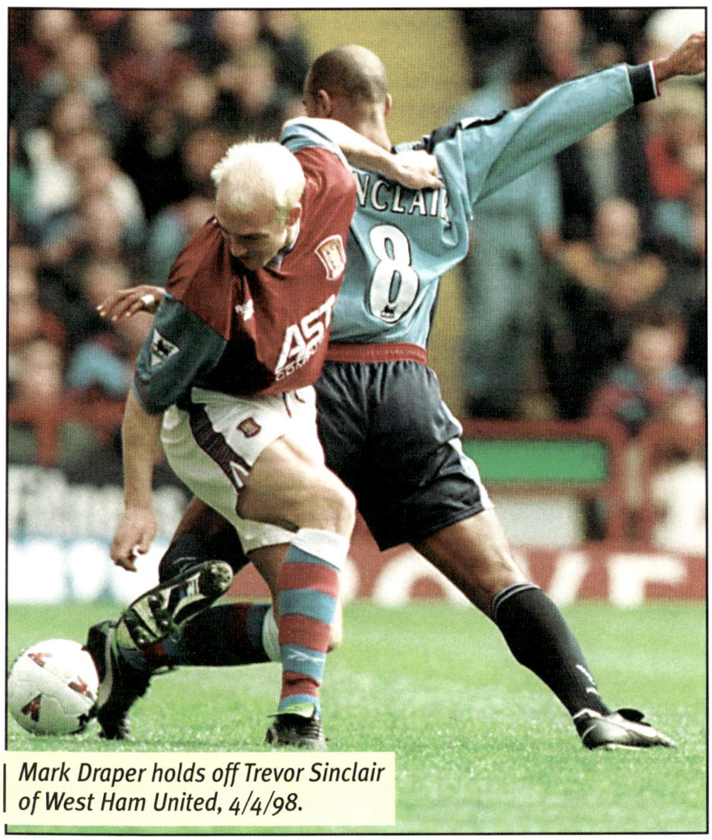

ALLSPORT

Mark Draper holds off Trevor Sinclair of West Ham United, 4/4/98.

Preferred team formation: 3–5–2
Biggest rivals: Birmingham City

Programme: Aston Villa News and Record
Programme Editor: Bernard Gallagher
Programme Price: £2.00
Bus routes to stadium: Nos 7, 11, 440

FANZINES

Heroes and Villains, PO Box 1703, Perry Barr, Birmingham B42 1UZ
The Holy Trinity, 216 Brandwood Road, Kings Heath, Birmingham B14 6LD
Witton Wag, PO Box 26, Wednesbury, WS10 9YT

CONTACT NUMBERS

(Tel code 0121)

- Main number 327 2299
- Fax 322 2107
- Ticket Information 327 5353
- Commercial Department 327 5399
- Commercial Fax 328 2099
- Club shop 327 2800
- Clubcall 0891 121 148
- Ticketline 0891 121 83448

LEADING PLAYERS

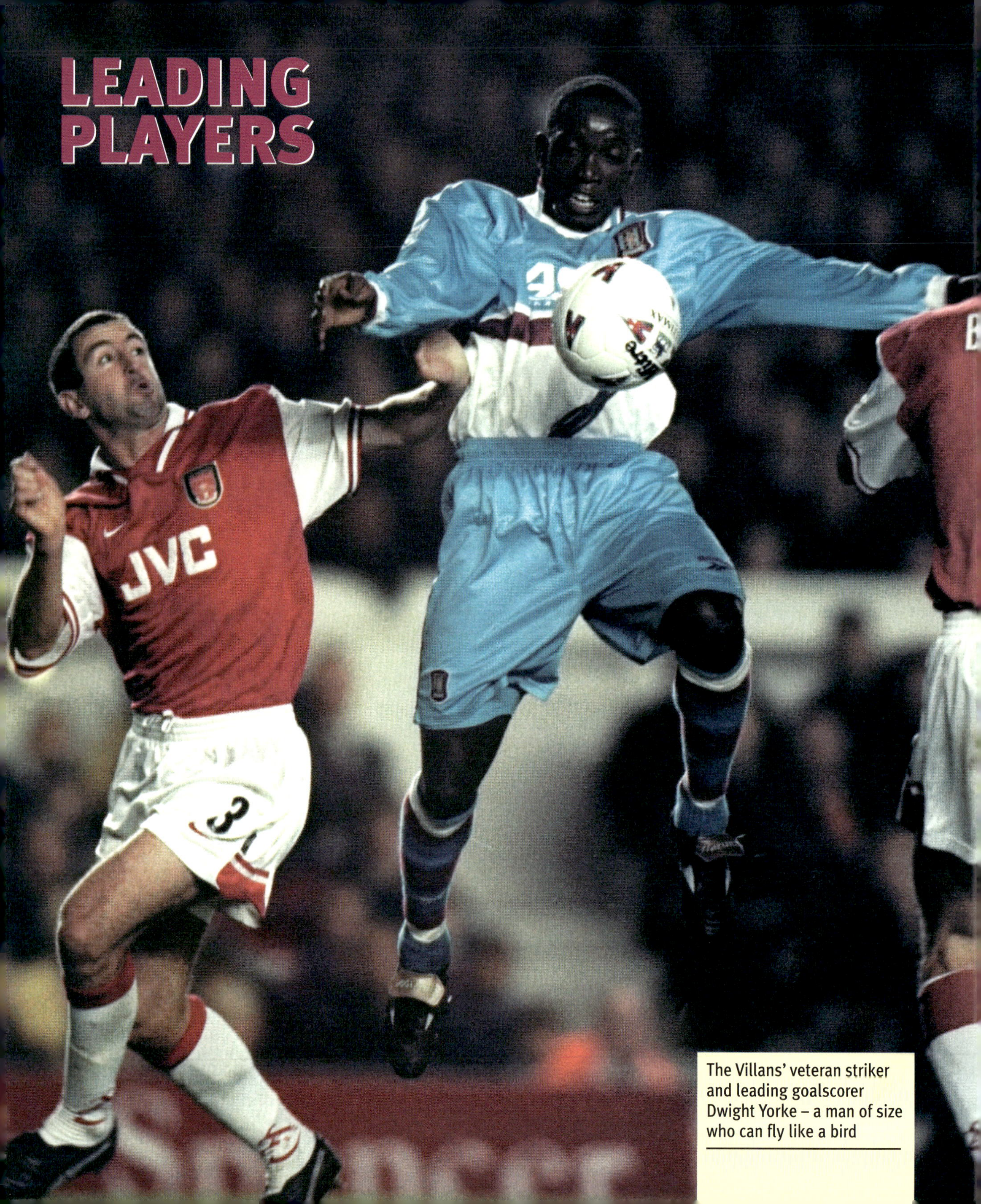

The Villans' veteran striker and leading goalscorer Dwight Yorke – a man of size who can fly like a bird

1997/98 SEASON TOP 10 GOALSCORERS

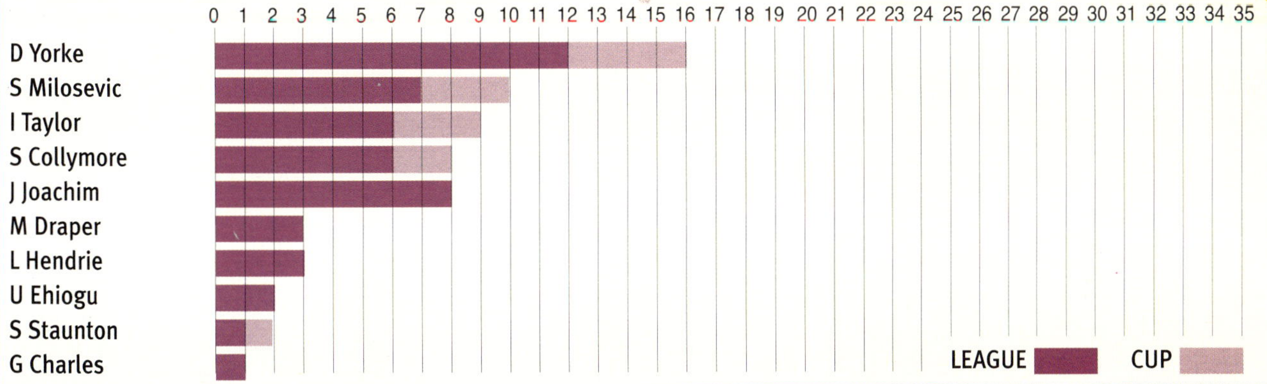

MOST LEAGUE APPEARANCES

PLAYER		APPEARANCES	SUBSTITUTE	GOALS
1	Ugo Ehiogu	37	0	2
2	Alan Wright	35	2	0
3	Simon Grayson	28	5	0
4	Gareth Southgate	32	0	0
5	Mark Draper	31	0	3
6	Ian Taylor	30	2	6
7	Mark Bosnich	30	0	0
8	Dwight Yorke	30	0	12
9	Steve Staunton	27	0	1
10	Julian Joachin	16	10	8
11	Stan Collymore	23	2	6
12	Fernando Nelson	21	4	0
13	Savo Milosevic	19	4	7
14	Riccardo Scimeca	16	5	0
15	Gary Charles	14	4	1
16	Lee Hendrie	13	4	3
17	Michael Oakes	8	0	0
18	Darren Byfield	1	6	0
19	Sasa Curcic	3	4	0
20	Gareth Barry	1	1	0

PLAYER STATISTICS

Record transfer fee paid:
Stan Collymore – £7,000,000 from Liverpool May 1997

Record transfer fee received:
David Platt – £5,500,000 from Bari July 1991

Oldest player: Ernie Callaghan, 39 years and 257 days against Grimsby Town, Division One, April 12th 1947

Youngest player: Jimmy Brown, 15 years and 349 days against Bolton Wanderers, September 17th 1969

International captains:
Andy Townsend (Eire), Vic Crowe (Wales)

Most capped player:
Paul McGrath, 51, Republic of Ireland (1990–96)

SQUAD

MARK BOSNICH

DOB: 13/1/72
Position: Goalkeeper
Squad number: 1
When joined club: February 1992 from Sydney Croatia
League Games played: 164
League Goals scored: 0
International caps: Australia (9)
League Debut: 18/4/92 v Nottingham Forest (A)

MICHAEL OAKES

DOB: 30/10/73
Position: Goalkeeper
Squad number: 13
When joined club: From Juniors July 1991
League Games played: 28
League Goals scored: 0
International caps: 0
League Debut: 17/8/96 v Sheffield Wednesday (A)

GARY CHARLES

DOB: 14/4/70
Position: Defender
Squad number: 2
When joined club: January 1995 from Derby County
League Games played: 68
League Goals scored: 2
International caps: England (2)
League Debut: 21/1/95 v Nottingham Forest (A)

UGO EHIOGU

DOB: 3/11/72
Position: Defender
Squad number: 5
When joined club: July 1991 from West Bromwich Albion
League Games played: 179
League Goals scored: 9
International caps: England (1)
League Debut: 24/8/91 v Arsenal (h)

ALLSPORT

Stan Collymore revving up for a run against West Ham United at Upton Park on 29/10/97. Unfotunately, the Villans didn't hold their own and went down to the Hammers 2–1.

Flying Dwight Yorke attempts a shot at Derby County's goal on 20/9/97. It must have helped, Aston won 2–1.

ALLSPORT

SIMON GRAYSON

DOB: 16/12/69
Position: Defender
Squad number: 16
When joined club: June 1997 from Leicester City
League Games played: 33
League Goals scored: 0
International caps: 0
League Debut: 13/8/97 v Blackburn (H)

DAVID HUGHES

DOB: 1/2/78
Position: Defender
Squad number: 19
When joined club: July 1996 from Trainee
League Games played: 7
League Goals scored: 0
International caps: 0
League Debut: 2/3/97 v Liverpool (H)

FERNANDO NELSON

DOB: 5/11/71
Position: Defender
Squad number: 15
When joined club: July 1996 from Sporting Lisbon
League Games played: 59
League Goals scored: 0
International caps: Portugal (5)
League Debut: 4/9/96 v Everton (A)

RICCARDO SCIMECA

DOB: 13/6/75
Position: Defender
Squad number: 20
When joined club: July 1993 from Trainee
League Games played: 50
League Goals scored: 0
International caps: 0
League Debut: 19/8/95 v Manchester United

Julian Joachim tussles with Derby County's Igor Stimac, 7/2/98

ALLSPORT

SASA CURCIC

DOB: 14/2/72
Position: Midfielder
Squad number: 18
When joined club: August 1996 from Bolton Wanderers
League Games played: 29
League Goals scored: 0
International caps: 0
League Debut: 24/8/96 v Derby County (H)

GARETH SOUTHGATE

DOB: 3/9/70
Position: Defender
Squad number: 4
When joined club: July 1995 from Crystal Palace
League Games played: 91
League Goals scored: 2
International caps: England (19)
League Debut: 19/8/95 v Manchester United (H)

MARK DRAPER

DOB: 11/11/70
Position: Midfielder
Squad number: 8
When joined club: July 1995 from Leicester City
League Games played: 96
League Goals scored: 5
International caps: 0
League Debut: 19/8/95 v Manchester United (H)

STEVE STAUNTON

DOB: 19/1/69
Position: Defender
Squad number: 3
When joined club: August 1991 from Liverpool
League Games played: 208
League Goals scored: 16
International caps: Republic of Ireland (68)
League Debut: August 1991

IAN TAYLOR

DOB: 4/6/68
Position: Midfielder
Squad number: 7
When joined club: December 1994
League Games played: 113
League Goals scored: 12
International caps: 0
League Debut: 26/12/94 v Arsenal (A)

ALAN WRIGHT

DOB: 28/9/71
Position: Defender
Squad number: 14
When joined club: March 1995 from Blackburn Rovers
League Games played: 121
League Goals scored: 3
International caps: 0
League Debut: 18/3/95 v West Ham United (H)

STAN COLLYMORE

DOB: 22/1/71
Position: Striker
Squad number: 11
When joined club: July 1997 from Liverpool
League Games played: 25
League Goals scored: 6
International caps: England (2)
League Debut: 9/8/97 v Leicester City (A)

Lee Hendrie looks a touch cold in the January weather as Aston VIlla go head-to-head with neighbouring West Brom in the FA Cup 5th round

ALLSPORT

DARREN BYFIELD

DOB: 29/9/76
Position: Striker
Squad number: 25
When joined club: August 1993 from trainee
League Games played: 7
League Goals scored: 0
International caps: 0
League Debut: 28/12/97 v Leeds United (A)

JULIAN JOACHIM

DOB: 20/9/74
Position: Striker
Squad number: 11
When joined club: February 1996 from Leicester City
League Games played: 26
League Goals scored: 4
International caps: 0
League Debut: 24/2/96 v Wimbledon (A)

SAVO MILOSEVIC

DOB: 2/9/73
Position: Striker
Squad number: 9
When joined club: July 1995 from Partizan Belgrade
League Games played: 86
League Goals scored: 28
International caps: Yugoslavia (18)
League Debut: 19/8/95 v Manchester United (H)

LEE HENDRIE

DOB: 18/5/77
Position: Midfielder
Squad number: 17
When joined club: From trainee May 1994
League Games played: 24
League Goals scored: 3
International caps: 0
League Debut: 23/12/95 v QPR (A)

DWIGHT YORKE

DOB: 3/11/71
Position: Striker
Squad number: 10
When joined club: December 1989 from Signal Hill
League Games played: 200
League Goals scored: 61
International caps: Trinidad & Tobago (15)
League Debut: 24/3/90 v Crystal Palace

1997/98 SEASON FINAL POSITIONS

POINTS 10 20 30 40 50 60 70 80 90 100 200 300 400 500

Club	Points	Goals	Average position in the Premier League since joining	Average position by points in the league since joining	Average position by goals in the league since joining
Arsenal	4543	6168	5	3	12
Aston Villa	4463	6549	6	4	1
Blackburn Rovers	4372	6183	4	8	11
Charlton Athletic	3259	4453	20	65	60
Chelsea	3758	5087	8	36	34
Coventry City	3196	4273	17	67	67
Derby County	4329	6249	10	10	8
Everton	4455	6306	16	5	6
Leeds United	3522	4475	7	43	58
Leicester City	4027	5796	14	24	19
Liverpool	4801	6457	2	1	3
Manchester United	4710	6402	1	2	5
Middlesbrough	3990	5615	19	26	26
Newcastle United	4308	6436	3	14	4
Nottingham Forest	4230	5707	15	19	22
Sheffield Wednesday	4231	5887	12	18	17
Southampton	3274	4545	18	61	53
Tottenham Hotspur	3794	5383	9	35	28
West Ham United	3369	3355	13	57	80
Wimbledon	1220	1259	11	88	88

3 Average position in the Premier League since joining

92 Average position by points in the league since joining — includes 2 points for a win and 3 points for a win

92 Average position by goals in the league since joining

1 Arsenal
2 Manchester United
3 Liverpool
4 Chelsea
5 Leeds United
6 Blackburn Rovers
7 Aston Villa
8 West Ham United
9 Derby County
10 Leicester City
11 Coventry City
12 Southampton
13 Newcastle United
14 Tottenham Hotspur
15 Wimbledon
16 Sheffield Wednesday
17 Everton
18 Bolton Wanderers (r)
19 Barnsley (r)
20 Crystal Palace (r)

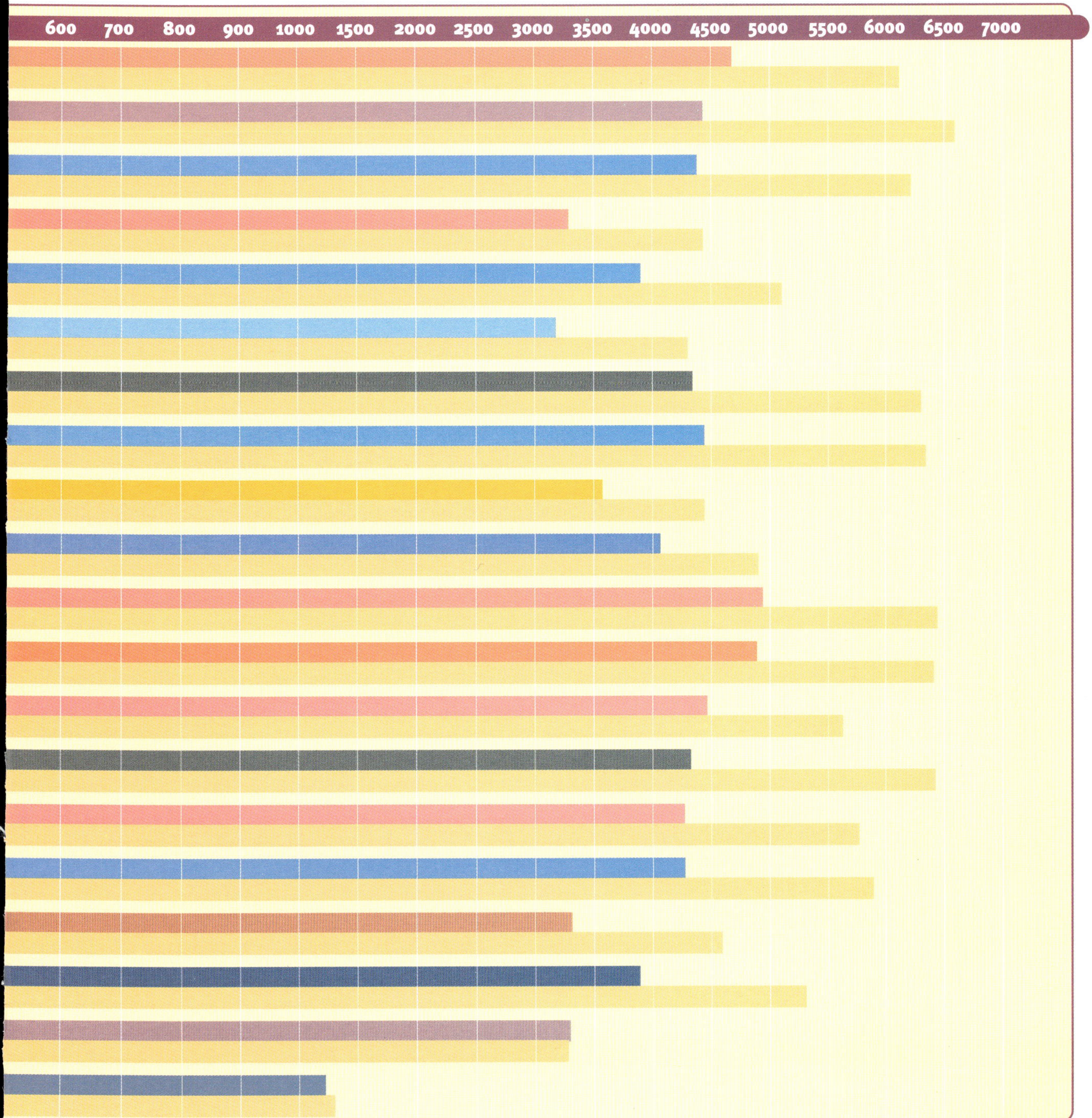

Aston Villa's total points since joining league................................ 4463

Villa Park: home of Aston Villa
AEROFILMS

SUPERCLUBS
UNOFFICIAL
SOCCER YEARBOOK 98/99

JULY 1998 – JUNE 1999 DIARY AND CLUB FIXTURES

Fixture dates are subject to change. FA Cup draws were not made at press-time.

THE STORY OF PREMIER LEAGUE SOCCER IN THE 1997/98 SEASON

FOR SUPPORTERS OF
ASTON VILLA

ENGLISH PREMIERSHIP CLUB ADDRESSES

ARSENAL
Arsenal Stadium, Highbury, London, N5 1BU
Main No: 0171 704 4000

ASTON VILLA
Villa Park, Trinity Road Stand, North Stand, Doug Ellis Road
Main No: 0121 327 2299

BLACKBURN ROVERS
Ewood Park, Blackburn, BB2 4JF
Main No: 01254 698888

CHARLTON ATHLETIC
The Valley, Floyd Road, Charlton, London, SE7 8BL
Main No: 0181 333 4000

CHELSEA
Stamford Bridge, Fulham Road, London, SW6 1HS
Main No: 0171 385 5545

COVENTRY CITY
Highfield Road Stadium, King Richard Street, Coventry, CV2 4FW
Main No: 01203 234000

DERBY COUNTY
Pride Park Stadium, Derby, DE24 8XL
Main No: 01332 667503

EVERTON
Goodison Park, Liverpool, L4 4EL
Main No: 0151 330 2200

LEEDS UNITED
Elland Road, Leeds, West Yorkshire, LS11 OES
Main No: 0113 226 6000

LEICESTER
Filbert Street, Leicester, LE2 7FL
Main No: 0116 291 5000

LIVERPOOL
Anfield Road, Liverpool. L4 OTH
Main No: 0151 263 2361

MANCHESTER UNITED
Old Trafford, Manchester
Main No: 0161 872 1661 & 0161 930 1968

MIDDLESBROUGH
Cellnet Riverside Stadium, Middlesbrough, Cleveland, TS3 6RS
Main No: 01642 877 700

NEWCASTLE UNITED
St James' Park, Newcastle-Upon-Tyne, NE1 4ST
Main No: 0191 201 8400

NOTTINGHAM FOREST
City Ground, Nottingham, NG2 5FJ
Main No: 0115 982 4444

SHEFFIELD WEDNESDAY
Hillsborough, Sheffield, S6 1SW
Main No: 0114 221 2121

SOUTHAMPTON
The Dell, Milton Road, Southampton, SO9 4XX
Main No: 01703 220505

TOTTENHAM HOTSPUR
White Hart Lane, 748 High Road, Tottenham, London, N17 OAP
Main No: 0181 365 5000

WEST HAM UNITED
Boleyn Ground, Green Street, Upton Park, London, E13 9AZ
Main No: 0181 542 2748

WIMBLEDON
Selhurst Park Stadium, Wimbledon
Main No: 0181 771 2233

ALL-CLUB LOCATIONS

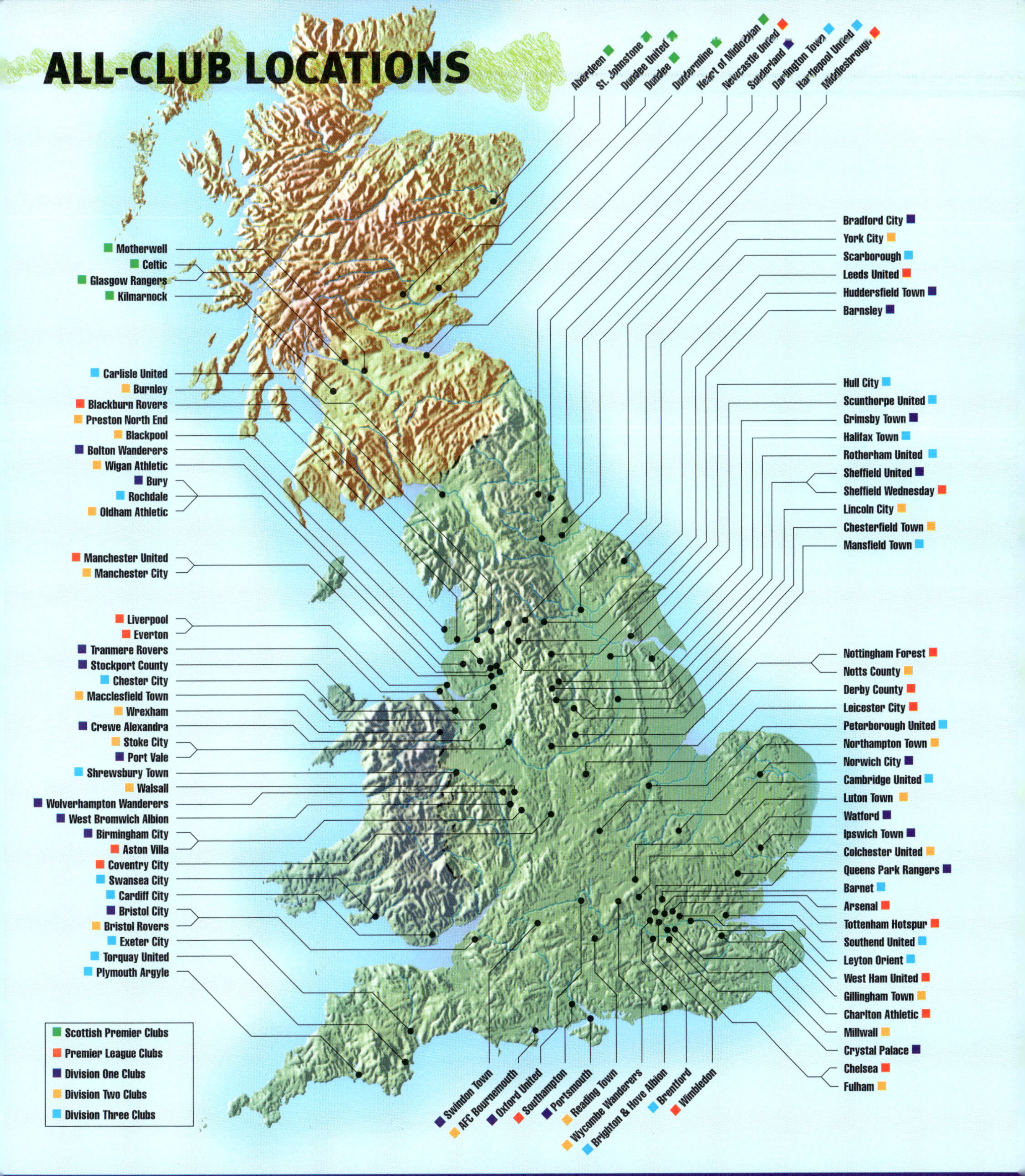

CALENDAR 1998

January

	M	T	W	T	F	S	S
1				1	2	3	4
2	5	6	7	8	9	10	11
3	12	13	14	15	16	17	18
4	19	20	21	22	23	24	25
5	26	27	28	29	30	31	

February

	M	T	W	T	F	S	S
5							1
6	2	3	4	5	6	7	8
7	9	10	11	12	13	14	15
8	16	17	18	19	20	21	22
9	23	24	25	26	27	28	

March

	M	T	W	T	F	S	S
9							1
10	2	3	4	5	6	7	8
11	9	10	11	12	13	14	15
12	16	17	18	19	20	21	22
13	23	24	25	26	27	28	29
14	30	31					

April

	M	T	W	T	F	S	S
14			1	2	3	4	5
15	6	7	8	9	10	11	12
16	13	14	15	16	17	18	19
17	20	21	22	23	24	25	26
18	27	28	29	30			

May

	M	T	W	T	F	S	S
18					1	2	3
19	4	5	6	7	8	9	10
20	11	12	13	14	15	16	17
21	18	19	20	21	22	23	24
22	25	26	27	28	29	30	31

June

	M	T	W	T	F	S	S
23	1	2	3	4	5	6	7
24	8	9	10	11	12	13	14
25	15	16	17	18	19	20	21
26	22	23	24	25	26	27	28
27	29	30					

July

	M	T	W	T	F	S	S
27			1	2	3	4	5
28	6	7	8	9	10	11	12
29	13	14	15	16	17	18	19
30	20	21	22	23	24	25	26
31	27	28	29	30	31		

August

	M	T	W	T	F	S	S
31						1	2
32	3	4	5	6	7	8	9
33	10	11	12	13	14	15	16
34	17	18	19	20	21	22	23
35	24	25	26	27	28	29	30
36	31						

September

	M	T	W	T	F	S	S
36		1	2	3	4	5	6
37	7	8	9	10	11	12	13
38	14	15	16	17	18	19	20
39	21	22	23	24	25	26	27
40	28	29	30				

October

	M	T	W	T	F	S	S
40				1	2	3	4
41	5	6	7	8	9	10	11
42	12	13	14	15	16	17	18
43	19	20	21	22	23	24	25
44	26	27	28	29	30	31	

November

	M	T	W	T	F	S	S
44							1
45	2	3	4	5	6	7	8
46	9	10	11	12	13	14	15
47	16	17	18	19	20	21	22
48	23	24	25	26	27	28	29
49	30						

December

	M	T	W	T	F	S	S
49		1	2	3	4	5	6
50	7	8	9	10	11	12	13
51	14	15	16	17	18	19	20
52	21	22	23	24	25	26	27
53	28	29	30	31			

UK Holiday   Scotland Holiday   N. Ireland Holiday   Not in Scotland

CALENDAR 1999

January

	M	T	W	T	F	S	S
1					1	2	3
2	4	5	6	7	8	9	10
3	11	12	13	14	15	16	17
4	18	19	20	21	22	23	24
5	25	26	27	28	29	30	31

February

	M	T	W	T	F	S	S
6	1	2	3	4	5	6	7
7	8	9	10	11	12	13	14
8	15	16	17	18	19	20	21
9	22	23	24	25	26	27	28

March

	M	T	W	T	F	S	S
10	1	2	3	4	5	6	7
11	8	9	10	11	12	13	14
12	15	16	17	18	19	20	21
13	22	23	24	25	26	27	28
14	29	30	31				

April

	M	T	W	T	F	S	S
14				1	2	3	4
15	5	6	7	8	9	10	11
16	12	13	14	15	16	17	18
17	19	20	21	22	23	24	25
18	26	27	28	29	30		

May

	M	T	W	T	F	S	S
18						1	2
19	3	4	5	6	7	8	9
20	10	11	12	13	14	15	16
21	17	18	19	20	21	22	23
22	24	25	26	27	28	29	30
23	31						

June

	M	T	W	T	F	S	S
23		1	2	3	4	5	6
24	7	8	9	10	11	12	13
25	14	15	16	17	18	19	20
26	21	22	23	24	25	26	27
27	28	29	30				

July

	M	T	W	T	F	S	S
27				1	2	3	4
28	5	6	7	8	9	10	11
29	12	13	14	15	16	17	18
30	19	20	21	22	23	24	25
31	26	27	28	29	30	31	

August

	M	T	W	T	F	S	S
31							1
32	2	3	4	5	6	7	8
33	9	10	11	12	13	14	15
34	16	17	18	19	20	21	22
35	23	24	25	26	27	28	29
36	30	31					

September

	M	T	W	T	F	S	S
36			1	2	3	4	5
37	6	7	8	9	10	11	12
38	13	14	15	16	17	18	19
39	20	21	22	23	24	25	26
40	27	28	29	30			

October

	M	T	W	T	F	S	S
40					1	2	3
41	4	5	6	7	8	9	10
42	11	12	13	14	15	16	17
43	18	19	20	21	22	23	24
44	25	26	27	28	29	30	31

November

	M	T	W	T	F	S	S
45	1	2	3	4	5	6	7
46	8	9	10	11	12	13	14
47	15	16	17	18	19	20	21
48	22	23	24	25	26	27	28
49	29	30					

December

	M	T	W	T	F	S	S
49			1	2	3	4	5
50	6	7	8	9	10	11	12
51	13	14	15	16	17	18	19
52	20	21	22	23	24	25	26
53	27	28	29	30	31		

Monday June 29 1998

Tuesday June 30 1998

Wednesday July 1 1998

Thursday July 2 1998

Friday July 3 1998

Saturday July 4 1998

Sunday July 5 1998

Monday July 6 1998

Tuesday July 7 1998

Wednesday July 8 1998

Thursday July 9 1998

Friday July 10 1998

Saturday July 11 1998

Sunday July 12 1998

9 August, 1997. After a wait of 110 years, Barnsley finally arrived in England's top division. And the press trotted out the predictable clichés. All the talk was of 'plucky Barnsley', dour but cheerful working class folk and brass bands. 'West Ham and Chelsea at home, Palace away – that's a nine-point start to the season,' offered optimistic professional Yorkshireman Michael Parkinson. Neil Redfearn nodded home Barnsley's Premiership opener in the ninth minute, but West Ham spoiled the party with two second-half strikes from Hartson and Lampard.

ALLSPORT

Barnsley fans enjoying the opening day of the Premiership

Teddy Sheringham's return to White Hart Lane on 10 August was an eventful occasion. The former Tottenham hero, now in the red of Manchester United after his £3.5 million summer switch, was booed and jeered mercilessly throughout by Spurs fans. Teddy had the opportunity to ram the taunts down their throats after Justin Edinburgh handled in the area in the 60th minute, but his spot-kick struck the post, much to the delight of the majority of the gathered 26,359. But Teddy's blushes were saved after United registered twice in two minutes. Nicky Butt scored from 12 yards in the 82nd minute, and 60 seconds later David Beckham's cross deflected off Ramon Vega and rolled past Ian Walker.

Teddy Sheringham missing the penalty at White Hart Lane

ALLSPORT

Monday July 13 1998

Tuesday July 14 1998

Wednesday July 15 1998

Thursday July 16 1998

Friday July 17 1998

Saturday July 18 1998

Sunday July 19 1998

Monday July 20 1998

Tuesday July 21 1998

Wednesday July 22 1998

Thursday July 23 1998

Friday July 24 1998

Saturday July 25 1998

Sunday July 26 1998

West Ham may have spoilt Barnsley's Premiership party on the opening day, but the South Yorkshire side took their revenge on the capital when they played against Crystal Palace at Selhurst Park on 12 August. Neil Redfearn, Barnsley's scorer against West Ham, struck a ferocious, dipping left-foot shot from 30 yards early in the second half and it proved enough for the Yorkshiremen to take the points north. New Palace hero Attilio Lombardo made little impression, despite his two-goal salvo at Goodison Park on the opening day. And manager Steve Coppell fined the Italian for turning up late. 'I didn't realise the traffic would be so thick in London,' offered Palace's own Bald Eagle.

ALLSPORT

Tykes starman, Neil Redfearn

The following day Aston Villa were put to the sword by a stunning first-half hat-trick from Blackburn's rejuvenated striker Chris Sutton. Roy Hodgson had instilled a real sense of belief in his short time as manager after the summer switch from Inter Milan, and Blackburn were rampant against an out-of-sorts Villa. Sutton registered three times in the opening 45 minutes and completely outshone his opposite number, seven-million-pound man Stan Collymore. With wingers Wilcox and Ripley raiding the flanks, Blackburn constantly offered a threat to the Villa defence. Sutton's first was the best of the three, the former Norwich man volleying home a Stuart Ripley centre from just inside the area.

Chris Sutton completing his first-half hat-trick

ALLSPORT

Monday July 27 1998

Tuesday July 28 1998

Wednesday July 29 1998

Thursday July 30 1998

Friday July 31 1998

Saturday August 1 1998

Sunday August 2 1998

Monday August 3 1998

Tuesday August 4 1998

Wednesday August 5 1998

Thursday August 6 1998

Friday August 7 1998

Saturday August 8 1998

Sunday August 9 1998

Tottenham secured their first victory of the season against Derby County on 23 August, much to the relief of their beleaguered boss Gerry Francis. With the gentlemen of the press predicting Francis as favourite to be the season's first Premiership managerial casualty, the Spurs boss was looking increasingly desperate, particularly with the signings of wingers David Ginola and José Dominguez. But Dominguez, a first-half substitute for injured Frenchman Ginola, shone on his debut, lifting the White Hart Lane faithful with his wizardry. Stefan Eranio's foul on the Portuguese winger led to the Spurs goal, Colin Calderwood heading home Sinton's resultant free-kick.

ALLSPORT

José Dominguez added zip to Spurs' early season

Barnsley's second home Premiership fixture on 24 August left them in no doubt about the task they faced in retaining their position in the top division. Chelsea's team of all-stars led the Yorkshiremen a merry dance with Gianluca Vialli helping himself to four goals in their 6–0 victory. Vialli, recalled in place of Mark Hughes, struck just before half-time and found the net three times after the interval in his finest performance since his transfer from Juventus. 'They toyed with us,' said Barnsley manager Danny Wilson, putting on as brave a face as he could muster.

Vialli had plenty to celebrate at the end of August 1997. Little did he know that within another seven months, he would have even more...

ALLSPORT

Monday August 10 1998

Tuesday August 11 1998

Wednesday August 12 1998

Thursday August 13 1998

Friday August 14 1998

Saturday August 15 1998

Aston Villa at Everton

Sunday August 16 1998

Monday August 17 1998

Tuesday August 18 1998

Wednesday August 19 1998

Thursday August 20 1998

Friday August 21 1998

Saturday August 22 1998

Sunday August 23 1998

Aston Villa at Middlesbrough

25 August: Blackburn's fixture against Sheffield Wednesday was hardly a mouth-watering prospect but it turned into one of the most astonishing Premiership games of the season. A fiery Blackburn ripped into the Wednesday defence from the off and after 24 minutes the score was 5–1 to Roy Hodgson's side. Scottish striker Kevin Gallacher scored twice in the first seven minutes before Wednesday's Carbone pulled one back. But the Lancashiremen had it wrapped up by half-time with strikes from Sutton, Wilcox and an own-goal from Graham Hyde. The second half wasn't without incident, either. Blackburn keeper John Filan was carried off with a broken arm, and Benito Carbone scored a brilliant 30-yarder before being sent off for headbutting.

ALLSPORT

Calm down Wrighty... again

27 August: Dennis Bergkamp continued his magnificent start to the season with a stunning hat-trick, but once again it was his strike partner Ian Wright who made all the headlines. Arsenal were winning 2–1 in the 90th minute but incredibly the score finished 3–3, with Leicester's Steve Walsh heading home deep into time added on. After the final whistle, there was an unseemly melee, which resulted in Wright, Patrick Vieira, Steve Walsh and Arsenal coach Pat Rice being reported to the FA. All were later cleared.

CALENDAR 1999

January

	M	T	W	T	F	S	S
1					1	2	3
2	4	5	6	7	8	9	10
3	11	12	13	14	15	16	17
4	18	19	20	21	22	23	24
5	25	26	27	28	29	30	31

February

	M	T	W	T	F	S	S
6	1	2	3	4	5	6	7
7	8	9	10	11	12	13	14
8	15	16	17	18	19	20	21
9	22	23	24	25	26	27	28

March

	M	T	W	T	F	S	S
10	1	2	3	4	5	6	7
11	8	9	10	11	12	13	14
12	15	16	17	18	19	20	21
13	22	23	24	25	26	27	28
14	29	30	31				

April

	M	T	W	T	F	S	S
14				1	2	3	4
15	5	6	7	8	9	10	11
16	12	13	14	15	16	17	18
17	19	20	21	22	23	24	25
18	26	27	28	29	30		

May

	M	T	W	T	F	S	S
18						1	2
19	3	4	5	6	7	8	9
20	10	11	12	13	14	15	16
21	17	18	19	20	21	22	23
22	24	25	26	27	28	29	30
23	31						

June

	M	T	W	T	F	S	S
23		1	2	3	4	5	6
24	7	8	9	10	11	12	13
25	14	15	16	17	18	19	20
26	21	22	23	24	25	26	27
27	28	29	30				

July

	M	T	W	T	F	S	S
27				1	2	3	4
28	5	6	7	8	9	10	11
29	12	13	14	15	16	17	18
30	19	20	21	22	23	24	25
31	26	27	28	29	30	31	

August

	M	T	W	T	F	S	S
31							1
32	2	3	4	5	6	7	8
33	9	10	11	12	13	14	15
34	16	17	18	19	20	21	22
35	23	24	25	26	27	28	29
36	30	31					

September

	M	T	W	T	F	S	S
36			1	2	3	4	5
37	6	7	8	9	10	11	12
38	13	14	15	16	17	18	19
39	20	21	22	23	24	25	26
40	27	28	29	30			

October

	M	T	W	T	F	S	S
40					1	2	3
41	4	5	6	7	8	9	10
42	11	12	13	14	15	16	17
43	18	19	20	21	22	23	24
44	25	26	27	28	29	30	31

November

	M	T	W	T	F	S	S
45	1	2	3	4	5	6	7
46	8	9	10	11	12	13	14
47	15	16	17	18	19	20	21
48	22	23	24	25	26	27	28
49	29	30					

December

	M	T	W	T	F	S	S
49			1	2	3	4	5
50	6	7	8	9	10	11	12
51	13	14	15	16	17	18	19
52	20	21	22	23	24	25	26
53	27	28	29	30	31		

Monday June 29 1998

Tuesday June 30 1998

Wednesday July 1 1998

Thursday July 2 1998

Friday July 3 1998

Saturday July 4 1998

Sunday July 5 1998

Monday July 6 1998

Tuesday July 7 1998

Wednesday July 8 1998

Thursday July 9 1998

Friday July 10 1998

Saturday July 11 1998

Sunday July 12 1998

9 August, 1997. After a wait of 110 years, Barnsley finally arrived in England's top division. And the press trotted out the predictable clichés. All the talk was of 'plucky Barnsley', dour but cheerful working class folk and brass bands. 'West Ham and Chelsea at home, Palace away – that's a nine-point start to the season,' offered optimistic professional Yorkshireman Michael Parkinson. Neil Redfearn nodded home Barnsley's Premiership opener in the ninth minute, but West Ham spoiled the party with two second-half strikes from Hartson and Lampard.

ALLSPORT

Barnsley fans enjoying the opening day of the Premiership

Teddy Sheringham's return to White Hart Lane on 10 August was an eventful occasion. The former Tottenham hero, now in the red of Manchester United after his £3.5 million summer switch, was booed and jeered mercilessly throughout by Spurs fans. Teddy had the opportunity to ram the taunts down their throats after Justin Edinburgh handled in the area in the 60th minute, but his spot-kick struck the post, much to the delight of the majority of the gathered 26,359. But Teddy's blushes were saved after United registered twice in two minutes. Nicky Butt scored from 12 yards in the 82nd minute, and 60 seconds later David Beckham's cross deflected off Ramon Vega and rolled past Ian Walker.

Kevin Gallacher masterfully handled by Des Walker

ALLSPORT

ALLSPORT

Above: David Hopkin brings Bremner-like attitude to Leeds and Scotland

Perennial World Cup qualifiers Scotland continued their impressive progress towards France 98 with a 4–1 victory over Belarus on 7 September. Leeds' David Hopkin, a second-half substitute for Scottish captain Gary McAllister of Coventry, opened his international account with two impressive strikes. In-form Blackburn Rovers striker Kevin Gallacher also scored a brace. The victory took Scotland back to the top of Group Four above Austria and ensured they would be guaranteed at least second spot and a play-off place.

1 September: Newly promoted Bolton Wanderers were one of two Premiership teams starting the season in a new stadium. But unlike Derby County, the Lancastrians had thus far been unable to christen the opulent £35 million Reebok Stadium with a goal. Surely with Everton the visitors their luck would change? In the 53rd minute, Bolton's Gerry Taggart nodded the ball just over the line, as TV replays later confirmed, but referee Stephen Lodge over-ruled. And the evening got worse for Bolton when their record signing, Robbie Elliot, was stretchered off with a broken leg. The game finished 0–0.

Right: Reebok Stadium

QUIZ 1 ABOUT ASTON VILLA

1 Aston Villa began life as:
a) Aston Villa Rugby Football Club?
b) Birmingham Cricket and Social Club?
c) Aston Villa Cricket Club?

2 Ian Hamilton's nickname is:
a) Chico?
b) Cheeky?
c) Cheeco?

3 Who is the Beatles 'connection' with Villa?
a) Former physio, Paul McCartney
b) Former youth team coach, George Harrison
c) Former manager, George Martin

ALLSPORT

4 Who scored the winner in the 1982 European Cup final victory?
a) Des Bremner
b) Peter Withe
c) Gordon Cowans

5 Before managing Leicester City, Brian Little had a spell at:
a) Doncaster Rovers?
b) Darlington Town?
c) Derby County?

6 Legendary Villa keeper Sam Hardy guested for which club during WWI?
a) Nottingham Forest
b) Liverpool
c) Birmingham City

7 Legend has it that Villa star Charlie Athersmith once played a game carrying:
a) A cigar?
b) A cane?
c) An umbrella?

8 Former Villa manager Dr Josef Venglos managed which national team?
a) Oman
b) Jordan
c) United Arab Emirates

9 Villa have several fanzines, which of the following is a real one?
a) Little or Nothing
b) Heroes and Villans
c) Claret and Stick

10 Ron Saunders, Tony Barton, Graham Turner... who is next in the sequence?
a) Graham Taylor
b) Josef Venglos
c) Ron Atkinson

Answers: 1.c 2.a 3.c 4.b 5.b 6.a 7.c 8.a 9.b 10.a

Monday August 24 1998

Tuesday August 25 1998

Wednesday August 26 1998

Thursday August 27 1998

Friday August 28 1998

Saturday August 29 1998
Aston Villa at Sheffield Wednesday

Sunday August 30 1998

Monday August 31 1998

Tuesday September 1 1998

Wednesday September 2 1998

Thursday September 3 1998

Friday September 4 1998

Saturday September 5 1998

Sunday September 6 1998

Paul Gascoigne produced his most impressive international performance since Euro 96 in England's emphatic 4–0 victory over Moldova in the World Cup qualifier on 10 September. Despite the poor quality of the opposition, Gascoigne dominated with a superb display of passing and dribbling, capped by a late goal. Paul Scholes opened England's account with a spectacular diving header from a David Beckham cross and Ian Wright weighed in with the other two. England went into the game knowing that if they beat Moldova, they would only need to draw against Italy in Rome, after the Italians failed to beat Georgia.

ALLSPORT

Paul Gascoigne scoring against Moldova

Leeds ended a run of three straight defeats with a victory over Blackburn Rovers in another astonishing game at Ewood Park on 14 September. Three weeks earlier, Rovers had slaughtered Sheffield Wednesday 7–2, but this time the team from the west side of the Pennines refused to roll over. All seven goals came in a frantic first 33 minutes as Leeds raced to a 4–3 lead that they held on to until the end. The best strikes came from Rod Wallace and Kevin Gallacher, the latter a flashing 25-yard drive. 'It was great for the fans but the standard of defending was awful from both teams,' said a relieved George Graham afterwards.

Rod Wallace, Leeds favourite, shows his class against Blackburn

ALLSPORT

Monday September 7 1998

Tuesday September 8 1998

Wednesday September 9 1998
Newcastle United at Aston Villa

Thursday September 10 1998

Friday September 11 1998

Saturday September 12 1998
Wimbledon at Aston Villa

Sunday September 13 1998

Monday September 14 1998

Tuesday September 15 1998

Wednesday September 16 1998

Thursday September 17 1998

Friday September 18 1998

Saturday September 19 1998
Aston Villa at Leeds United

Sunday September 20 1998

A big week for British teams in Europe began with one of the most eagerly awaited games for years, when Celtic met Liverpool at Parkhead in the first round of the UEFA Cup on 16 September. Liverpool whizzkid Michael Owen stunned the 48,526 crowd when he finished with coolness beyond his years in the sixth minute. But Celtic replied with two second-half strikes and seemed certain to take a 2–1 lead to Anfield for the second leg. That was until Steve McManaman picked up the ball well inside his own half and proceeded to dribble the length of the field before slotting past Jonathan Gould (a recent signing from Bradford and Celtic's third-choice keeper) into the Celtic net.

ALLSPORT

'Macca' disrupts the Celtic-Liverpool camaraderie

Newcastle United finally realised their dream of playing in the Champions' League when they welcomed visitors Barcelona to St James' Park on 17 September. Roared on by a capacity crowd, the Geordies tore into the Spanish giants with Tino Asprilla scoring two first-half goals to give them a 2–0 lead at the interval. Asprilla completed his hat-trick after the break, but when Barcelona scored two late goals, it was Newcastle who found themselves praying for the whistle. 'The best game in recent times in Europe,' reckoned Kenny Dalglish.

Tino's biggest game of the season. Against Barca he was awesome

ALLSPORT

Monday September 21 1998

Tuesday September 22 1998

Wednesday September 23 1998

Thursday September 24 1998

Friday September 25 1998

Saturday September 26 1998
Derby County at Aston Villa

Sunday September 27 1998

Monday September 28 1998

Tuesday September 29 1998

Wednesday September 30 1998

Thursday October 1 1998

Friday October 2 1998

Saturday October 3 1998
Aston Villa at Coventry City

Sunday October 4 1998

Republic of Ireland skipper Roy Keane suffered a devastating knee injury in Manchester United's first defeat of the campaign at Leeds on 27 September. Keane fell to the ground after a clumsy challenge on Leeds' Norwegian international Alf-Inge Haaland. Keane was shown the yellow card by referee Martin Bodenham and promptly limped off only to find the injury would keep him out for the rest of the season. The hard-fought Roses battle was settled in the 34th minute when Leeds' defender David Wetherall rose above Gary Pallister and headed Gary Kelly's free-kick past Schmeichel.

ALLSPORT

Youth versus Experience: Danny Cadamarteri struggles with Nigel Winterburn

In the meeting with leaders Arsenal at Goodison Park, Everton fans finally had something to cheer about after their miserable start to the season. With neighbours Liverpool bringing youngsters of the likes of Michael Owen through the ranks, the blue half of Merseyside rose to acclaim two 17-year-olds of their own in the 2–2 draw with the Londoners. Arsenal raced to a 2–0 lead at the interval with goals from Wright and Overmars but Everton fought back after the break. First, rookie defender Michael Ball headed in from close range and, seven minutes later, Goodison rose to greet a new hero when the dreadlocked Cadamarteri equalised from close range.

Youth and Experience: Gary Kelly leaves Paul Scholes on the deck as Leeds defeat the old enemy

ALLSPORT

1998 OCTOBER 5 – OCTOBER 18

Monday October 5 1998

Tuesday October 6 1998

Wednesday October 7 1998

Thursday October 8 1998

Friday October 9 1998

Saturday October 10 1998

Sunday October 11 1998

Monday October 12 1998

Tuesday October 13 1998

Wednesday October 14 1998

Thursday October 15 1998

Friday October 16 1998

Saturday October 17 1998

Aston Villa at West Ham United

Sunday October 18 1998

Manchester United had begun their Champions' League campaign with an impressive 3–0 victory away at FC Kosice, but Alex Ferguson knew the real test was to come. On 1 October Italian champions Juventus, European Cup finalists last season, winners the year before, arrived at Old Trafford in confident mood but were completely outplayed by a rampant United. In a stunning display of passing and movement, the champions of England put on their finest performance for years with goals from Sheringham, Scholes and Giggs securing the 3–1 win. Alex Ferguson even forgot to check his stopwatch.

ALLSPORT

Giggs... all set for another season of achievement

After leading Stockport County to promotion, manager Dave Jones found himself in demand with Premiership Southampton after Graeme Souness' acrimonious Saints walkout. But Jones soon found the Premiership going tough, and after 10 games, Southampton were rooted to the bottom of the table. And then West Ham visited the Dell on 4 October. Both teams huffed and puffed through the first half in front of a watching Glenn Hoddle, but the Saints broke the Hammers' resistance when substitute Ostenstad poked in from close range. Kevin Davies, the Saints' new signing from last season's FA Cup dream-merchants Chesterfield, extended the lead before Jason Dodd settled the issue with a 30-yard pile driver.

Youth and Experience: Gary Kelly leaves Paul Scholes on the deck as Leeds defeat the old enemy

ALLSPORT

Monday October 5 1998

Tuesday October 6 1998

Wednesday October 7 1998

Thursday October 8 1998

Friday October 9 1998

Saturday October 10 1998

Sunday October 11 1998

Monday October 12 1998

Tuesday October 13 1998

Wednesday October 14 1998

Thursday October 15 1998

Friday October 16 1998

Saturday October 17 1998

Aston Villa at West Ham United

Sunday October 18 1998

Manchester United had begun their Champions' League campaign with an impressive 3–0 victory away at FC Kosice, but Alex Ferguson knew the real test was to come. On 1 October Italian champions Juventus, European Cup finalists last season, winners the year before, arrived at Old Trafford in confident mood but were completely outplayed by a rampant United. In a stunning display of passing and movement, the champions of England put on their finest performance for years with goals from Sheringham, Scholes and Giggs securing the 3–1 win. Alex Ferguson even forgot to check his stopwatch.

ALLSPORT

Giggs... all set for another season of achievement

After leading Stockport County to promotion, manager Dave Jones found himself in demand with Premiership Southampton after Graeme Souness' acrimonious Saints walkout. But Jones soon found the Premiership going tough, and after 10 games, Southampton were rooted to the bottom of the table. And then West Ham visited the Dell on 4 October. Both teams huffed and puffed through the first half in front of a watching Glenn Hoddle, but the Saints broke the Hammers' resistance when substitute Ostenstad poked in from close range. Kevin Davies, the Saints' new signing from last season's FA Cup dream-merchants Chesterfield, extended the lead before Jason Dodd settled the issue with a 30-yard pile driver.

'Carlton, you're supposed to hold the ball up, not scorer Jason Dodd!'

ALLSPORT

Paul Ince, in Terry Butcher mould, looks on as Italy fail to score

ALLSPORT

11 October: England's trip to Rome for the World Cup showdown with Italy proved one of the most memorable nights in recent football history. Needing just a point to be sure of qualifying for France 98, England produced one of their most assured performances ever to secure a draw at the Olympic Stadium. With Newcastle's David Batty and Liverpool's Paul Ince outstanding in midfield, England soaked up the pressure and guaranteed their qualification. There was controversy, though, as the treatment meted out to travelling supporters by Italian police was universally deplored. 'The provocation the England fans had was unbelievable,' claimed England manager Glenn Hoddle, as the extent of the trouble was revealed in the aftermath.

The repercussions from the Rome game continued to resonate all week, only being taken off the back-page headline positions by Glenn Hoddle's shock divorce announcement. On the events in Rome, politicians from all hues of the political spectrum weighed in with their opinions, and David Mellor made the trip to Italy to confront Rome's chief of police on behalf of the BBC's Watchdog consumer programme. The major worry however was not for the fans but for England's World Cup 2006 final bid. With Euro 96 and its policing receiving praise from all over the world, but with memories of Hysel and Italia 90 still at the forefront of European minds, any bid from this side of the channel was anything but firm in the balance.

ALLSPORT

English fans... but this time the terrace terror was in uniform

Quiz 2 Referee Quiz

1 In the event of the crossbar being broken, or somehow moved from its position, and replacing it is not possible, the referee will:

a) Allow another item such as a taut rope to be used as a replacement.
b) Allow play to continue without a crossbar
c) Abandon the game.

2 The minimum height for a corner flagpole is

a) 1.5m
b) .5m
c) 1.75m

3 A goal is scored from a throw-in. Does the referee:

a) Disallow it?
b) Use his discretion?
c) Allow the goal?

4 Only eight players appear for one side in a professional eleven-a-side game. Does the referee:

a) Abandon the game?
b) Allow the game to continue?
c) Allow non-registered players to fill-in and continue the game?

5 An outfield player swaps positions with the goalkeeper without informing the referee. The ref notices while the ball is in play. Does he?

a) Immediately send both players off?
b) Allow play to continue and wait for a natural break?
c) Immediately book both players?

6 The ref gives a direct free kick in your penalty area. One of your players kicks it back to the keeper who misses the ball completely. The ball goes into your own net! Does the referee:

a) Order the free kick to be taken again?
b) Award a goal to the opposition?
c) Award a corner-kick to the opposition?

7 What is wrong with the picture at the top of a penalty shoot-out?

a) The goalkeeper of the team taking the kick is in the centre circle with the rest of his teammates. Should he be standing on the 18-yard line?
b) The goalkeeper has his arms raised when they should be still and by his side?
c) The referee is in the penalty area causing a distraction when he should be standing on the 18-yard line.

8 There are three minutes left in a game when one manager decides to make a substitution. Two minutes later the ball goes out of play, it takes one minute to make the substitution. Does the referee:

a) Blow the whistle for full-time when the player enters the field?
b) Book the manager for time-wasting?
c) Add time on for the substitution?

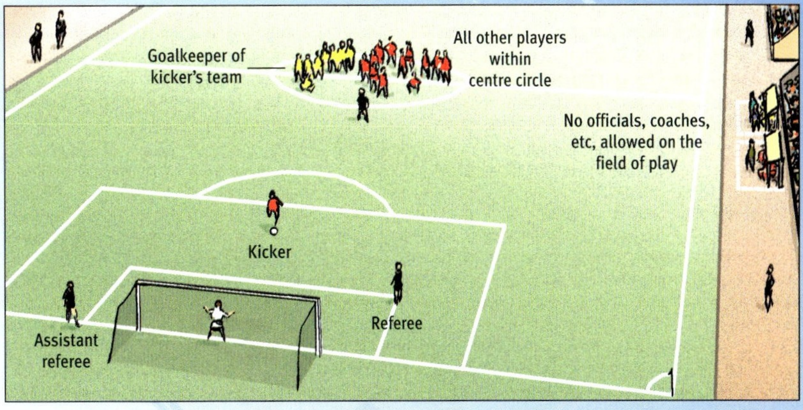

9 What is wrong with this picture of the 'Technical Area'?

a) Nothing.
b) There are no markings showing the correct distance.
c) The distances shown are wrong.

10 In this picture, does the referee:

a) Give the goal?
b) Not give the goal?
c) Give a drop-ball?

Answers: 1.c 2.a 3.a 4.b 5.b 6.c 7.a 8.c 9.a 10.b

Monday October 19 1998

Tuesday October 20 1998

Wednesday October 21 1998

Thursday October 22 1998

Friday October 23 1998

Saturday October 24 1998
Leicester City at Aston Villa

Sunday October 25 1998

Monday October 26 1998

Tuesday October 27 1998

Wednesday October 28 1998

Thursday October 29 1998

Friday October 30 1998

Saturday October 31 1998
Aston Villa at Chelsea

Sunday November 1 1998

The Merseyside derby was as hotly contested as ever but it was the blue half of Liverpool who emerged victorious. Everton's 2–0 win on 18 October was capped by another fine display from new Goodison hero, 17-year-old Danny Cadamarteri and it relieved the pressure on beleaguered boss Howard Kendall. 'Liverpool are a quality side who make it difficult for you – now we need to maintain this standard,' said a delighted Kendall after the game. For Liverpool and Roy Evans, though, the defeat left them in mid-table and struggling to keep up the pace set by Arsenal and Manchester United.

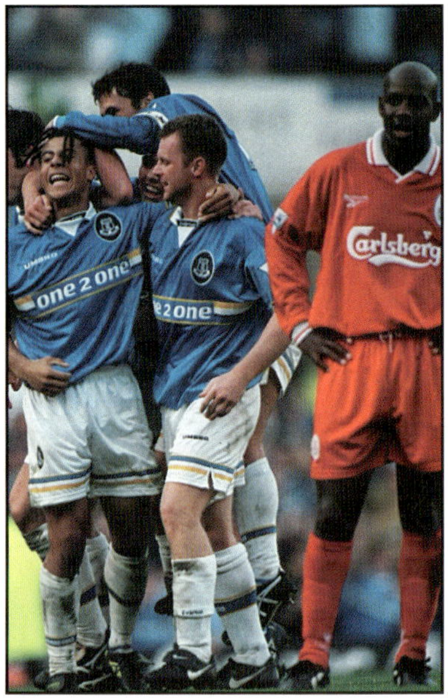

ALLSPORT

Cadamarteri makes the Scouse Derby a day to remember for the Blues

Newcastle slumped to their biggest ever defeat under Kenny Dalglish when they went down 4–1 to Leeds at Elland Road. Leeds' recent run had seen them beat pace-setters Blackburn and Manchester United and they kept up their impressive form by racing to a 3–0 lead at the interval. Wetherall headed home just after the break to seal victory before Gillespie scored a late consolation for the visitors. 'It's the worst defeat by far since I came here and I hope it's just a blip, because we had no indication of this beforehand,' said a disappointed Dalglish.

Into the frying pan eh Kenny? Dalglish tries to manage the Toon

ALLSPORT

Monday November 2 1998

Tuesday November 3 1998

Wednesday November 4 1998

Thursday November 5 1998

Friday November 6 1998

Saturday November 7 1998

Tottenham Hotspur at Aston Villa

Sunday November 8 1998

Monday November 9 1998

Tuesday November 10 1998

Wednesday November 11 1998

Thursday November 12 1998

Friday November 13 1998

Saturday November 14 1998

Aston Villa at Southampton **FA Cup round 1**

Sunday November 15 1998

Chelsea survived a massive scare in their second-round European Cup Winners' Cup-tie against the battling Norwegians of Tromso on 23 October. The Blues were lucky to come away only 3–2 down, thanks to two late Gianluca Vialli goals, in a game played in blizzard conditions at a stadium some 200 miles inside the Arctic Circle. The referee stopped the tie three times so that ground staff could brush snow off the touchlines and penalty areas. 'We had to play into the blizzard, for 45 minutes, with the snow straight into our eyes so we couldn't see at all,' said a rueful then-manager Gullit after the game.

ALLSPORT

Andy Cole celebrating his hat-trick

Premier League champions Manchester United put Barnsley to the sword with a devastating display of finishing. Andy Cole rediscovered his goal touch with a supreme first-half hat-trick in a United display that had boss Alex Ferguson purring: 'Performances like that happen once or twice a season.' Barnsley fans, once famous for their 'it's just like watching Brazil' chant, were forced to change the lyrics to, 'it's just like watching Grange Hill'. But manager Danny Wilson remained ebullient after the game. 'There was nothing between the teams apart from seven goals,' he chirped.

The second-half blizzard in Tromso

ALLSPORT

Monday November 16 1998

Tuesday November 17 1998

Wednesday November 18 1998

Thursday November 19 1998

Friday November 20 1998

Saturday November 21 1998
Liverpool at Aston Villa

Sunday November 22 1998

Monday November 23 1998

Tuesday November 24 1998

Wednesday November 25 1998

Thursday November 26 1998

Friday November 27 1998

Saturday November 28 1998
Aston Villa at Nottingham Forest

Sunday November 29 1998

Coventry moved into a comfortable mid-table berth by beating Wimbledon 2–1 at Selhurst Park on 27 October. After narrowly escaping relegation on the last day of the previous season, Gordon Strachan's Sky Blues were aiming for loftier heights the following term. Goals from Darren Huckerby and Man of the Match Dion Dublin secured victory before a crowd of 11,201, the lowest Premiership gathering of the day. 'I must enjoy this job as I haven't taken to drink, my wife is still with me and there are not too many grey hairs,' said a delighted Strachan after the game.

ALLSPORT

Dion Dublin, surrounded by Light Blues, adds another goal to his tally

Promoted Bolton's first six matches at their new Reebok Stadium saw only three goals but no fewer than five sendings off. Stan Collymore, Alan Todd, Nathan Blake and Gary Pallister were all shown the red card (Pallister's was later quashed on appeal) before Robbie Fowler received his marching orders for elbowing Per Frandson. The dismissal crowned a mixed day for the England striker who had shot Liverpool into the lead in the first minute, before Blake pegged them back with an 84th minute equaliser. 'We all know if anyone raises their hands they have to go,' commented Bolton boss Colin Todd afterwards. And he should know.

Alan Thompson offers Robbie Fowler some consolation as Karl-Heinz Riedle remonstrates with referee Dermott Gallacher

Monday November 30 1998

Tuesday December 1 1998

Wednesday December 2 1998

Thursday December 3 1998

Friday December 4 1998

Saturday December 5 1998

Manchester United at Aston Villa

FA Cup round 2

Sunday December 6 1998

Monday December 7 1998

Tuesday December 8 1998

Wednesday December 9 1998

Thursday December 10 1998

Friday December 11 1998

Saturday December 12 1998

Arsenal at Aston Villa

Sunday December 13 1998

Leeds produced an astonishing comeback to defeat Derby County 4–3 at Elland Road on 8 November. Substitutes Jimmy Floyd Hasselbaink and Lee Bowyer combined in the last minute and Bowyer rifled home the winner with a firm left-foot strike. This result would have been unthinkable after a first half-hour that saw Jim Smith's side race into a 3–0 lead. Dean Sturridge scored twice before Asanovic converted a spot-kick and the game looked all but over. But Leeds rallied and pulled back two goals before half-time. Then Hasselbaink converted a late penalty before Bowyer struck. George Graham was understandably pleased at the comeback. 'It just goes to show the camaraderie here. After the first 20 minutes I thought we were superb – the better team by far.'

ALLSPORT

Rodney Wallace adds to one of the most exciting Leeds versus Derby clashes in decades

Billed as the 'biggest Premiership game of the season so far,' Arsenal's 9 November attempt to close the gap on leaders Manchester United was not without incident. The Gunners marched into a 2–0 lead with impressive strikes from French duo Nicolas Anelka and Patrick Vieira before being pegged back before half-time by a brace from Teddy Sheringham. United then had a legitimate claim for a penalty refused by referee Martin Bodenham before Peter Schmeichel was hit by a missile thrown from the crowd. The perpetrator was later arrested. David Platt, in for the suspended Emmanuel Petit, secured the points for Arsenal with a flashing header, although most observers felt United's performance warranted at least a share of the points. Alex Ferguson later described the referee as 'a master of not seeing anything'.

Henning Berg discovers Peter Schmeichel's contact lenses in the game against Arsenal at Highbury

ALLSPORT

ALLSPORT

It's a Liverpool double as Steve MacManaman celebrates Robbie Fowler's first goal for England

England continued their build-up to World Cup France 98 with a comfortable 2–0 friendly victory over a poor Cameroon. The Africans were a pale shadow of the side that had performed so well on the world stage over the past few years. England's best player on the night was Manchester United striker Paul Scholes who capped an excellent performance with a superbly manufactured chip after great work from Paul Gascoigne. Minutes later, Robbie Fowler nodded home a David Beckham cross to make the game safe. Glenn Hoddle was gushing in his praise of Scholes afterwards: 'He could be the jewel in the crown because he can score goals and is proving it at club and international level.'

Leicester City's bright start to the season suffered a blip as they were beaten at Filbert Street by perennial party poopers Wimbledon on 15 November. The Dons registered in the 50th minute when Marcus Gayle's header was judged to have crossed the line after it hit the crossbar and rebounded out. It was all the more annoying for the Foxes because victory would have seen them leapfrog into the heady heights of 5th in the table, above the likes of Liverpool and Newcastle. But once again, Wimbledon confounded their critics, and their opposition, to steal the three points.

Right: Marcus Gayle beats Matt Eliot to the ball as the Dons hunt the Foxes

QUIZ 3 ABOUT ASTON VILLA

1 What is the club nickname of Aston Villa?
- a) The Villans
- b) The Comedians
- c) The Astons

2 In what year did Villa finish runners-up in the Premiership?
- a) 1992-93
- b) 1993-94
- c) 1994-95

3 Who is the most capped player ever to play for Aston Villa?
- a) David Platt
- b) Paul McGrath
- c) Gareth Southgate

ALLSPORT

4 In what year was the club formed?
- a) 1899
- b) 1874
- c) 1882

5 What is the record attendance at Villa Park?
- a) 76,588
- b) 56,344
- c) 73,293

6 Which club competition have Aston Villa never won?
- a) The Cup Winners' Cup
- b) The World Club Championship
- c) The European Cup

7 In may 1997 Villa paid Liverpool how much for Stan Collymore?
- a) £6,500,000
- b) £7,000,000
- c) £7,500,000

8 To which Spanish club did David Platt move in July 1991?
- a) Sampdoria
- b) Inter Milan
- c) Bari

9 Which player has made the most league appearances for Aston Villa?
- a) Harry Hampton
- b) Charlie Aitken
- c) 'Pongo' Waring

10 How many times have Aston Villa won the League Championship?
- a) Five
- b) Six
- c) Seven

Answers: 1.a 2.a 3.b 4.b 5.a 6.a 7.b 8.c 9.b 10.c

Monday December 14 1998

Tuesday December 15 1998

Wednesday December 16 1998

Thursday December 17 1998

Friday December 18 1998

Saturday December 19 1998

Sunday December 20 1998

Monday December 21 1998
Aston Villa at Charlton Athletic

Tuesday December 22 1998

Wednesday December 23 1998

Thursday December 24 1998

Friday December 25 1998

Saturday December 26 1998
Aston Villa at Blackburn Rovers

Sunday December 27 1998

Barnsley sprung the Premiership's biggest upset of 1997 when they beat Liverpool 1–0 at Anfield on 22 November. Ashley Ward, out for the previous month suffering from viral meningitis, scored the game's only goal when Andy Liddell's cross bounced off Patrik Berger's shins allowing Ward to convert from close range. 'The boss asked me on Thursday if I wanted to play. To score at Liverpool of all places makes it complete,' said the delighted Barnsley striker. Liverpool had plenty of chances to equalise, with Karl-Heinz Riedle the main culprit. 'We did no defending,' was Roy Evans' stinging verdict.

ALLSPORT

'BFR' is back in the 'best job in the world' at Hillsborough

Ron Atkinson's return to club management with Sheffield Wednesday got off to a great start with a fine 2–0 victory over Premiership frontrunners Arsenal. In his previous managerial stint at Wednesday, Atkinson delivered the Owls' first major trophy in 56 years when they lifted the League Cup. It ended in acrimony when 'Big' Ron left to manage Aston Villa. But all was forgotten as Sheffield Wednesday's biggest crowd of the season to date, 34,373, turned up to see Arsene Wenger's Arsenal comfortably beaten. Goals from Andy Booth and Guy Whittingham sealed Wednesday's victory and Atkinson was understandably jubilant. 'I can see real quality in this team,' he said afterwards.

Barnsley pull a famous away victory out of the bag with an Ashley Ward goal

ALLSPORT

Monday December 28 1998
Sheffield Wednesday at Aston Villa

Tuesday December 29 1998

Wednesday December 30 1998

Thursday December 31 1998

Friday January 1 1999

Saturday January 2 1999
FA Cup round 3

Sunday January 3 1999

Monday January 4 1999

Tuesday January 5 1999

Wednesday January 6 1999

Thursday January 7 1999

Friday January 8 1999

Saturday January 9 1999
Aston Villa at Middlesbrough

Sunday January 10 1999

29 November: Goals from Ramon Vega and David Ginola provided Tottenham's new manager Christian Gross with the perfect start and sank beleaguered Everton further into the relegation mire. Hundreds of fans remained in the Goodison stands after the match to call for the Toffees' chairman, Peter Johnson, to relinquish control of the club. And the defeat sent Everton to rock bottom in the Premiership table. Swiss star Vega opened the scoring in the 72nd minute, nodding home an Andy Sinton cross after Ruel Fox had flicked the ball on. Then David Ginola ran the Everton defence ragged before firing past Southall with a decisive left foot strike.

ALLSPORT

Christian Gross hops from Grasshoppers to Spurs

30 November: Manchester United comprehensively outplayed second-placed Blackburn to stretch their lead at the top of the Premiership. A brace from Ole Solskjaer and own-goals from Stefan Henchoz and Jeff Kenna left the chasing pack in no doubt as to the task they faced in toppling the champions. Solskjaer opened the scoring in the 18th minute, neatly chesting the ball down before converting from close range. And early in the second half, the Norwegian outpaced the Rovers' defence to power in a right-foot strike from the edge of the area. To compound Blackburn's misery, England forward Chris Sutton was sent from the field of play after lunging at Nicky Butt.

Baby-faced he may be, but Ole Gunnar Solskjaer showed immense early maturity for Manchester United

ALLSPORT

Monday January 11 1999

Tuesday January 12 1999

Wednesday January 13 1999

Thursday January 14 1999

Friday January 15 1999

Saturday January 16 1999
Everton at Aston Villa

Sunday January 17 1999

Monday January 18 1999

Tuesday January 19 1999

Wednesday January 20 1999

Thursday January 21 1999

Friday January 22 1999

Saturday January 23 1999
FA Cup round 4

Sunday January 24 1999

V Andy Cole struck twice to settle Manchester United's Saturday morning, 6 December, showdown with bitter rivals Liverpool at Anfield. The in-form United striker opened his account early in the second half after a mistake by Bjorn Kvarme. But Liverpool equalised nine minutes later after Nicky Butt clattered Michael Owen in the box – Robbie Fowler converted the spot-kick. However, the Premiership leaders were not to be denied. David Beckham struck a beautiful 22-yard free-kick over the Liverpool wall and past David James, and then Cole settled the issue, slotting home neatly from close range. 'We won't give up but, realistically, our best bet for honours is now in the cups,' said a disappointed Roy Evans afterwards.

ALLSPORT

Andy Cole's second goal against Liverpool

➤ Tottenham's second match under the stewardship of Christian Gross ended in their heaviest home defeat since 1935. Ruud Gullit's Chelsea struck six times, with five goals coming after the break. Norwegian striker Tor Andre Flo helped himself to a hat-trick, the third a delightful chip over Spurs keeper Ian Walker. 'That was the easiest match I have experienced in English football,' said the delighted Flo. 'I was surprised how Spurs collapsed after our second goal.' But it was back to the drawing board for former Grasshoppers Zurich manager Gross.

Chelsea's team spirit builds yet again as Tor Andre Flo is buried under an international bundle

ALLSPORT

Monday January 25 1999

Tuesday January 26 1999

Wednesday January 27 1999

Thursday January 28 1999

Friday January 29 1999

Saturday January 30 1999

Aston Villa at Newcastle United

Sunday January 31 1999

Monday February 1 1999

Tuesday February 2 1999

Wednesday February 3 1999

Thursday February 4 1999

Friday February 5 1999

Saturday February 6 1999

Blackburn Rovers at Aston Villa

Sunday February 7 1999

On 13 December, Barnsley's former Newcastle hitman John Hendrie rescued a welcome point for the Yorkshiremen against Kenny Dalglish's side. Hendrie fired home a 20-yard bullet past Shaka Hislop in the 75th minute after two goals from Newcastle winger Keith Gillespie had looked like keeping up Newcastle's faltering Premiership challenge. Barnsley took the lead in the ninth minute when Neil Redfearn curled the ball into the top corner, before Gillespie struck twice, either side of half-time. 'There's been an all-round improvement,' said the relieved Barnsley boss Danny Wilson afterwards. 'I think we're learning.'

ALLSPORT

Ian Walker, Spurs' high-flying keeper...

Tottenham Hotspur's majestic Frenchman David Ginola lifted the gloom at White Hart Lane as Spurs coasted to a 3–0 victory over Danny Wilson's Barnsley on 20 December. Ginola capped a wonderful first-half display with two goals as Spurs raced to a three-goal lead in the first 18 minutes. Allen Nielson opened the scoring in the sixth minute when he latched onto a through-ball from Darren Anderton before dispatching a low drive past Lars Leese. But it was Ginola who basked in the limelight, orchestrating everything from the centre of Spurs' midfield. But once again, Danny Wilson was left lamenting his back line. 'We shot ourselves in the foot by making schoolboy errors,' he said afterwards.

Pistone of Newcastle bears down on Barnsley's Nicky Eaden

ALLSPORT

ALLSPORT

John Newsome looks on as Vialli shows the commitment for which he is rightfully known

20 December: Ron Atkinson's new Sheffield Wednesday charges were hammered 4–1 at Hillsborough by high-flying Chelsea's foreign legion. Goals by Dan Petrescu, Vialli, Flo and a converted spot-kick from Frank Leboeuf ensured that Ruud Gullit's side took the spoils. Romanian Petrescu converted from just inside the 18-yard area in the 30th minute, and by the time Pembridge opened Wednesday's account, Chelsea had added two more. The best goal of the game was scored by Norwegian striker Tore Andre Flo when he swaggered through the Sheffield defence before firing past Pressman. 'I'm sure Chelsea have had harder practice matches than that,' fumed Big Ron after Wednesday's abject surrender.

Premiership leaders Manchester United overcame Howard Kendall's Everton with embarrassing ease at Old Trafford on Boxing Day. United hardly left first gear in a 2–0 victory which extended their run of consecutive league victories to six and afforded them a six-point gap at the Premiership summit. Henning Berg opened United's account in the 14th minute, converting from close range after David Beckham's cross was headed back across goal by Ronny Johnson. And then Andy Cole fashioned a superb second, chipping Everton keeper Thomas Myhre from 25 yards. 'It was an embarrassing 90 minutes for us. It was men against boys and the scoreline flatters us,' said a dejected Howard Kendall afterwards.

Quiz 4 About The Premier League

1. **Who won the first ever Premiership title?**
   a) Leeds United
   b) Blackburn Rovers
   c) Manchester United

2. **Who holds the record for the least number of points accumulated in a Premiership season?**
   a) Swindon Town
   b) Ipswich Town
   c) Bolton Wanderers

3. **Who was the Premiership top scorer in the 1993-94 season?**
   a) Alan Shearer
   b) Andy Cole
   c) Teddy Sheringham

4. **Who was footballer of the year that same season?**
   a) Alan Shearer
   b) Andy Coal
   c) Teddy Sheringham

Manchester United's Nicky Butt eye on the ball... and the prize

Allsport

5. **In which stadium did Blackburn Rovers clinch the 1994-95 title?**
   a) Upton Park
   b) Ewood Park
   c) Anfield

6. **During which Premiership season was Arsenal manager George Graham banned from football for a year for receiving 'bungs'?**
   a) 1993-94
   b) 1994-95
   c) 1995-96

7. **Which Premiership club were Manchester United playing in April 1996 when they famously abandoned their grey kit at half-time?**
   a) Coventry City
   b) Southampton
   c) Sheffield Wednesday

8. **Which company signed a deal to sponsor the Premiership in February 1993?**
   a) Carling
   b) Littlewoods
   c) Bass

9. **Which foreign star scored a hat-trick on his Premiership debut in 1996?**
   a) Patrick Berger
   b) Gianfranco Zola
   c) Fabrizio Ravanelli

10. **Who was the first player to score a hat-trick in the Premiership?**
    a) Alan Shearer
    b) Eric Cantona
    c) Ian Wright

Answers: 1.c 2.b 3.a 4.a 5.c 6.c 7.b 8.c 9.c 10.b

Monday February 8 1999

Tuesday February 9 1999

Wednesday February 10 1999

Thursday February 11 1999

Friday February 12 1999

Saturday February 13 1999
Leeds United at Aston Villa FA Cup round 5

Sunday February 14 1999

Monday February 15 1999

Tuesday February 16 1999

Wednesday February 17 1999

Thursday February 18 1999

Friday February 19 1999

Saturday February 20 1999
Aston Villa at Wimbledon

Sunday February 21 1999

Tottenham and Arsenal shared the spoils in the North London derby at White Hart Lane on 28 December. But the draw left Spurs languishing in the relegation zone with fellow strugglers Barnsley and Everton. The majority of the 29,000 faithful were hoping that Jürgen Klinsmann could score the goal to sink Arsene Wenger's Gunners. And although the Germany captain didn't oblige, he did have a hand in Spurs' opener. In the 28th minute, Ruel Fox crossed from the right, Klinsmann flicked on and Allan Nielson converted smartly from close range. But Arsenal were not to be denied a share of the points. On the hour, Ray Parlour struck from just inside the box, his shot deflecting off Ramon Vega past Walker. 'Tottenham were really pumped up,' commented Arsene Wenger afterwards. 'Their determination really surprised in the first 30 minutes.'

ALLSPORT

Paul Ince – close marking is no longer a problem

3 January 1998, and Liverpool slumped to an embarrassing home defeat at the first hurdle in the FA Cup against Coventry. The Reds were booed off the park by the Anfield faithful after Gordon Strachan's impressive Coventry had burst through Liverpool's leaky rearguard almost at will. Roy Evans could not have imagined such a reverse when Jamie Rednapp's free-kick curled around the wall and into the net in the seventh minute. But on the stroke of half-time, Darren Huckerby cut a swathe through the Liverpool defence before slotting home from an acute angle. Dion Dublin added another midway through the second half before Paul Telfer ensured Coventry would be in the bag for the fourth round.

Klinsmann's shock return to White Hart Lane was yet another attempt to lift Spurs' nose-diving season

ALLSPORT

Monday February 22 1999

Tuesday February 23 1999

Wednesday February 24 1999

Thursday February 25 1999

Friday February 26 1999

Saturday February 27 1999
Coventry City at Aston Villa

Sunday February 28 1999

Monday March 1 1999

Tuesday March 2 1999

Wednesday March 3 1999

Thursday March 4 1999

Friday March 5 1999

Saturday March 6 1999
Aston Villa at Derby County FA Cup quarter-finals

Sunday March 7 1999

Unibond League part-timers Emley almost pulled off a sensational result against West Ham on 3 January. The Yorkshire village side (population 1,800), whose numbers include the obligatory fireman and postman, rocked the Premiership outfit with a battling display against the odds. And their moment of glory came 11 minutes into the second half when chemical plant worker Paul David headed home, to equalise Frank Lampard's fourth-minute opener. The non-leaguers were just nine minutes from forcing a replay when John Hartson nodded home from close range to seal victory. 'We have murdered Newcastle and Aston Villa here, but Emley gave us a much rougher ride,' said relieved England defender Rio Ferdinand afterwards.

ALLSPORT

Not quite a hat-trick for Giggs, but it kept Spurs well in check

10 January: Ryan Giggs capped a fine individual performance by scoring a brace against a Tottenham side boasting the recently returned German striker Jürgen Klinsmann. Alex Ferguson rested Nicky Butt, moved Paul Scholes to central midfield and gave Ole Solskjaer an outing on the left wing, but these changes made no difference to Manchester United's fluid rhythm. Giggs opened the scoring just before half-time with a solid drive from close range after Spurs keeper Baardson failed to hold a Beckham cross. The Welshman headed home another Beckham centre after the break to extend United's lead at the top of the Premiership.

Rio Ferdinand, the West Ham youth finally got to play for England after a drive-in with the law

ALLSPORT

Monday March 8 1999

Tuesday March 9 1999

Wednesday March 10 1999

Thursday March 11 1999

Friday March 12 1999

Saturday March 13 1999
Aston Villa at Tottenham Hotspur

Sunday March 14 1999

Monday March 15 1999

Tuesday March 16 1999

Wednesday March 17 1999

Thursday March 18 1999

Friday March 19 1999

Saturday March 20 1999
Chelsea at Aston Villa

Sunday March 21 1999

Vauxhall Conference side Stevenage Borough almost pulled off a sensational FA Cup result against Premiership giants Newcastle on 24 January. The hullabaloo surrounding Stevenage's right to stage the game at Broadhall Way failed to take the edge off a hard fought cup tie, as the Vauxhall Conference side bravely fought out a 1–1 draw. But it looked bleak for Stevenage as early as the third minute when Alan Shearer comfortably headed home Keith Gillespie's cross. It was the England striker's first goal since his return from six months on the sidelines. But the Conference side took the game to Newcastle for the remainder of the half, Guiliano Grazioli's close-range strike just reward for their efforts.

ALLSPORT

Another goal for the Cottee family scrapbook

On 31 January, Leicester City caused one of the shocks of the season when they defeated champions Manchester United 1–0 at Old Trafford, thus ending United's unbeaten home record. Leicester's veteran striker Tony Cottee latched onto a Garry Parker through ball in the 20th minute and slid the ball past Peter Schmeichel from close range. Cottee, famous for logging every goal in his personal scrapbook, was only in the side because Ian Marshall was out injured. 'We got what we deserved,' commented a rueful Alex Ferguson afterwards. 'We were too casual, particularly in the first half.'

Guiliano Grazioli's giant-stalling, if not killing, goal took the gingerbread off Newcastle's day

ALLSPORT

Monday March 22 1999

Tuesday March 23 1999

Wednesday March 24 1999

Thursday March 25 1999

Friday March 26 1999

Saturday March 27 1999

Sunday March 28 1999

Monday March 29 1999

Tuesday March 30 1999

Wednesday March 31 1999

Thursday April 1 1999

Friday April 2 1999

Saturday April 3 1999

West Ham United at Aston Villa

Sunday April 4 1999

Struggling Tottenham Hotspur upset the form book with an amazing 3–0 victory away at Blackburn Rovers on 7 February. Christian Gross, Spurs' Swiss manager had had little to shout about in his unsteady reign until this decisive victory at Ewood Park. Nicola Berti, Tottenham's midfield signing from Inter Milan, opened the scoring on 37 minutes, knocking the ball past Tim Flowers from close range. But although the majority of chances fell to Blackburn, Spurs extended their lead in the last minute when substitute Chris Armstrong struck a low drive from the edge of the box before Ruel Fox made the points safe in injury time. 'A lot has been said about Tottenham but we showed what we can do,' said a relieved Chris Armstrong, after three months out injured.

ALLSPORT

Sol Campbell makes life interesting for Blackburn's Damien Duff

A resurgent Arsenal overcame Chelsea 2–0 in a hard fought London derby at Highbury the next day. Two first-half goals from the Gunners' 21-year-old midfield sensation Stephen Hughes settled the issue, and earned him a new contract in the process. As early as the fourth minute, Nicolas Anelka latched onto a careless back pass by Frank Leboeuf, only to see his shot well saved by Ed de Goey. But the ball rebounded back into the area and Hughes slammed home an unstoppable left-foot shot from 16 yards. And just before half-time, Hughes was the first to react after Chelsea failed to clear a corner kick, the youngster nodding home inside the six-yard box. Little did Chelsea boss Ruud Gullit know he would get the sack a week later.

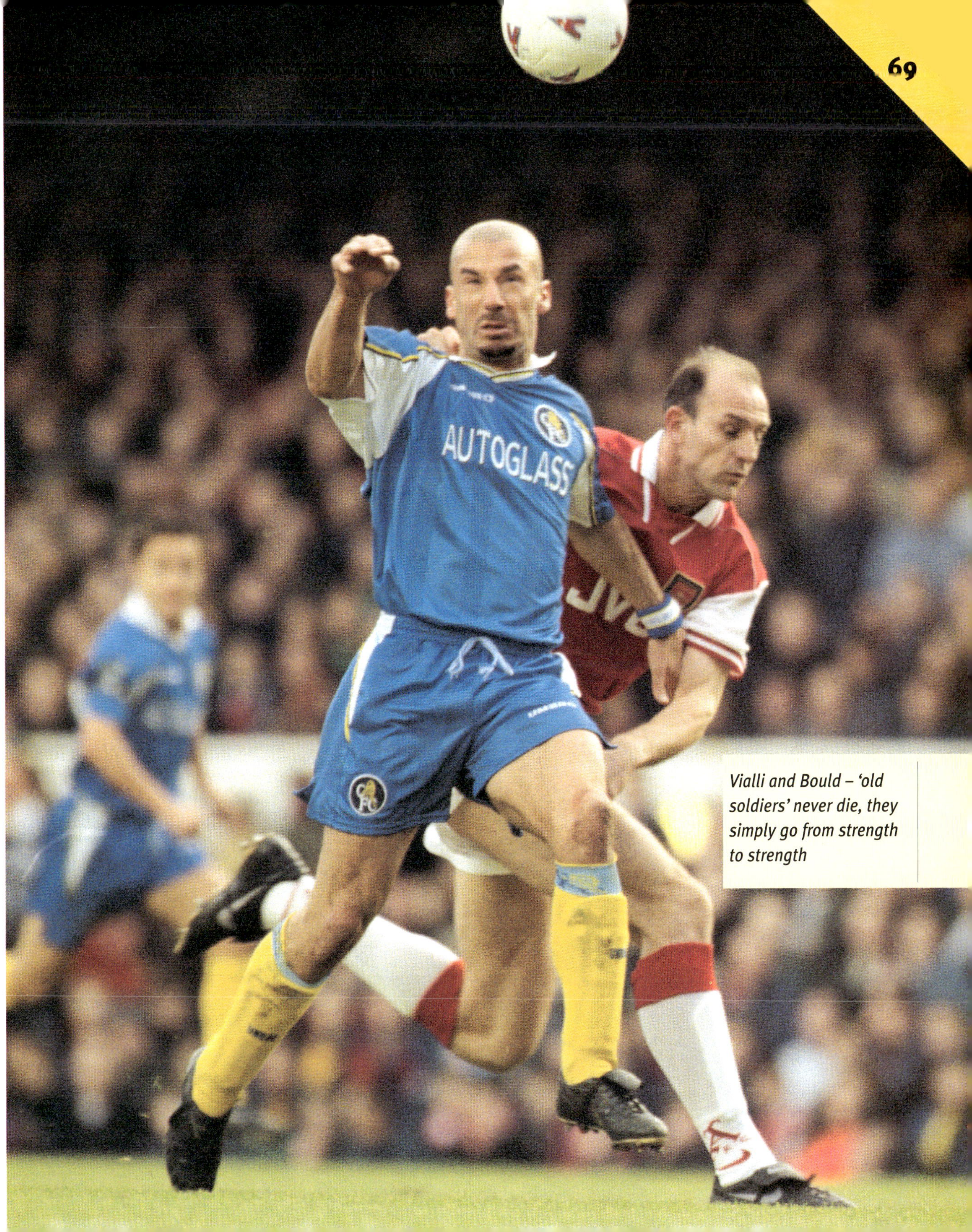

Vialli and Bould – 'old soldiers' never die, they simply go from strength to strength

Liverpool's precocious teenage striker Michael Owen capped the finest week of his career with a first senior hat-trick against Sheffield Wednesday at Hillsborough. The youngster, crowned 'Man of the Match' in England's 2–0 reverse against Chile at Wembley just three days previously, helped Liverpool salvage a point after they had trailed 3–1. Goals by Di Canio, Carbone and Andy Hinchcliffe looked set to secure victory for Ron Atkinson's Wednesday but it was Owen who took centre stage with two stunning late goals. 'Michael's frightening,' said Kevin Pressman, after Owen's devasting trio. 'Every keeper in the world will – believe me – worry about him.'

Paul Ince with his shooting boots on bemuses the Sheffield Wednesday defence yet again

Club-record signing Viorel Moldovan fired Coventry City into the last eight of the FA Cup against Aston Villa on Valentine's Day. The £3.25 million Romanian striker came off the bench to send Coventry's fans into Sky Blue heaven – it was their first victory at Villa Park after 25 unsuccessful attempts. Gordon Strachan's side were the better team throughout and deserved their victory over a lacklustre Villa, whose only genuine moment of class came after keeper Mark Bosnich pulled off a remarkable reflex save, volleying away Soltvedt's strike on goal. 'The winning goal was not just about getting into the last eight of the FA Cup, it was a claim for a first team place,' said a determined Moldovan afterwards.

Mark Bosnich dives to stop Moldovan's shot

Quiz 5 Referee Quiz

1 According to FIFA, what is the minimum length of a pitch used in an international game?
- a) 90 metres
- b) 95 metres
- c) 100 metres

2 What is the acceptable pressure of a football?
- a) 0.6 to 1.1 atmospheres
- b) 0.5 to 1.25 atmospheres
- c) 0.75 to 2 atmospheres

3 Is the red attacking number 10 offside in this Diagram?

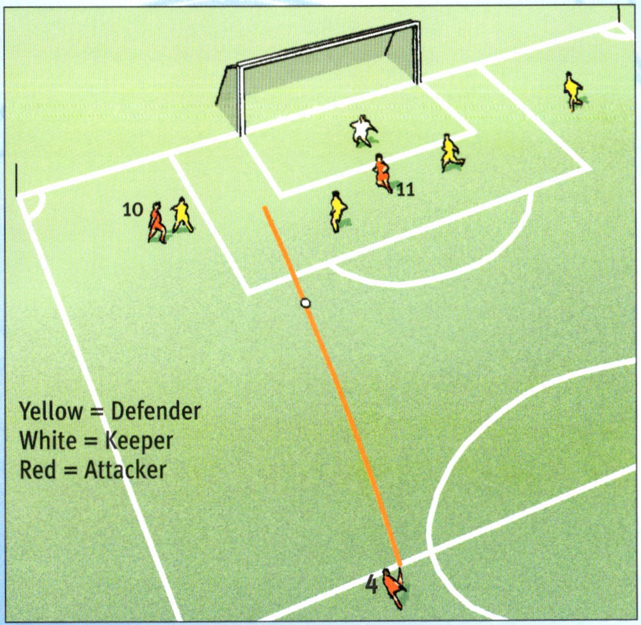

- a) No
- b) Yes
- c) Yes, but he's not interfering with play

4 When needs to go to penalties, who decides which end they are to be taken from?
- a) A toss of a coin before the game begins
- b) The referee decides
- c) A toss of a coin before the penalties are taken

5 If, during a penalty shoot-out, the keeper is injured and all substitutes have been used already, who replaces the keeper?
- a) A substitute keeper
- b) No one
- c) One of the outfield players

6 Your free-kick specialist takes a corner by flicking the ball in the air and curling it into the goal. What does the referee do?
- a) Awards the goal as fair
- b) Awards an indirect free-kick to the opposition (the corner taker is only allowed to touch the ball once until another player touches it).
- c) Awards a direct free-kick to the opposition (the corner taker is only allowed to touch the ball once until another player touches it).

7 Your keeper takes a free-kick but trips and the ball doesn't make it out of the area. What should the ref do?
- a) Has it taken again
- b) Allows play to continue
- c) Awards an indirect free-kick to the opposition

8 An opposition player persistently stands nose-to-nose with one of your team who is trying to take a throw-in, what should the referee do?
- a) Get the opposition player to stand 10-yards back
- b) Award an indirect free-kick to your team
- c) Caution the opposition player and give him a yellow card

9 What is the referee awarding in this Diagram?
- a) An indirect free-kick
- b) A corner
- c) A direct free-kick

10 If an indirect free-kick goes straight into the goal, what should the referee do?
- a) Have the kick re-taken
- b) Award an indirect free-kick to the opposition
- c) Award a goal kick

Answers: 1.c 2.a 3.a 4.b 5.c 6.b 7.a 8.c 9.a 10.c

Monday April 5 1999
Aston Villa at Leicester City

Tuesday April 6 1999

Wednesday April 7 1999

Thursday April 8 1999

Friday April 9 1999

Saturday April 10 1999
Southampton at Aston Villa **FA Cup semi-finals**

Sunday April 11 1999

Monday April 12 1999

Tuesday April 13 1999

Wednesday April 14 1999

Thursday April 15 1999

Friday April 16 1999

Saturday April 17 1999
Aston Villa at Liverpool

Sunday April 18 1999

Coventry condemned Danny Wilson's Barnsley to another cruel Premiership defeat on 21 February. Dion Dublin settled the issue in the 89th minute, converting a controversial spot-kick after he had been challenged in the 18 yard area by Peter Markstedt. Although Barnsley felt hard done by the decision, both Darren Huckerby and George Boateng had chances to settle the issue long before the penalty was awarded. Dublin's 17th goal of the campaign left his manager Gordon Strachan in a quandary about where to play him. 'Dion wants to be a forward because there's nothing like scoring goals, but in the long term centre-half may be his best position,' said the Sky Blues' boss.

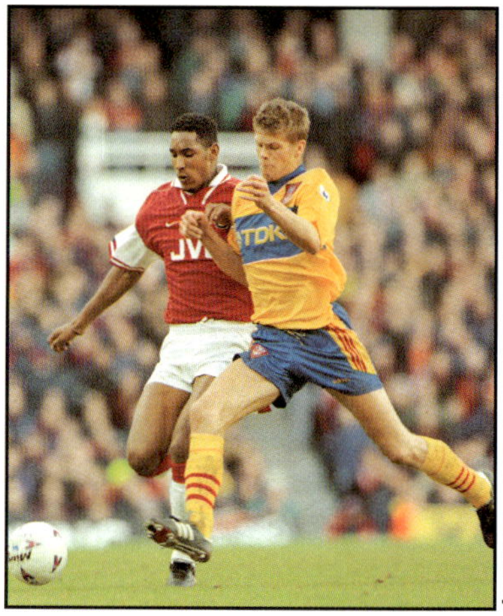

ALLSPORT

Patrick Vieira – strength, skill and style in an Arsenal shirt

The same day, Wimbledon outfought a disappointing Aston Villa side at Selhurst Park to move above Brian Little's men in the Premiership. Jason Euell opened the scoring in the 10th minute and Carl Leaburn extended the Dons' lead half an hour later, heading home neatly in the six-yard box. Although Savo Milosevic pulled a goal back on the stroke of half-time, any hope Villa had of rescuing a point disappeared when he limped off shortly after the break. 'There is no point in sitting down and feeling sorry for ourselves – we have just got to get on with it,' said Villa skipper Gareth Southgate afterwards. But for beleaguered boss Brian Little, it was one defeat too many. He resigned just days later.

Stan-the-Man out-leaps Wimbledon's Jones and Perry, can he see Brian Little leaving by the side entrance?

ALLSPORT

1999 APRIL 19 – MAY 2

Monday April 19 1999

Tuesday April 20 1999

Wednesday April 21 1999

Thursday April 22 1999

Friday April 23 1999

Saturday April 24 1999
Nottingham Forest at Aston Villa

Sunday April 25 1999

Monday April 26 1999

Tuesday April 27 1999

Wednesday April 28 1999

Thursday April 29 1999

Friday April 30 1999

Saturday May 1 1999
Aston Villa at Manchester United

Sunday May 2 1999

V Manchester United returned to the scene of their emphatic FA Cup victory to inflict another defeat over Chelsea at Stamford Bridge on 28 February. And United's winner came from an unlikely source. In the 31st minute, Philip Neville, playing on unfamiliar territory on the right side of midfield, popped up to slot the ball neatly past Dmitri Kharine. The Blues' player boss Gianluca Vialli, in only his third game at the helm, failed to lift Chelsea despite his presence on the field from the start. But he was full of praise for Ferguson's side afterwards. 'On the counter attack they are like the great European sides,' he enthused. 'One minute you are in their area, the next they break out and score.'

ALLSPORT

England versus Italy as Philip Neville battles with Roberto de Matteo in Manchester United's demolition of Chelsea at Stamford Bridge

> Chris Sutton scored a sparkling hat-trick against Leicester City at Ewood Park to remind Glenn Hoddle of his World Cup credentials. Sutton, who had refused to play for the England B team after being omitted from the senior squad, struck twice in the first half and completed his hat-trick soon after half-time with a superb chip over Kasey Keller. Leicester scored three late goals but Rovers held on for the points. 'You don't have to be a genius to work out that I haven't done my chances any good,' said Sutton after the game. 'But I believe in what I did and that's just as important to me.'

Chris Sutton's claim to the ball is stronger than his claim to an England place now

ALLSPORT

Monday May 3 1999

Tuesday May 4 1999

Wednesday May 5 1999

Thursday May 6 1999

Friday May 7 1999

Saturday May 8 1999
Charlton Athletic at Aston Villa

Sunday May 9 1999

Monday May 10 1999

Tuesday May 11 1999

Wednesday May 12 1999

Thursday May 13 1999

Friday May 14 1999

Saturday May 15 1999

Sunday May 16 1999
Aston Villa at Arsenal

14 March: Manchester United's slump in form continued when Arsenal arrived at Old Trafford for an 11.15 a.m. kick-off and deservedly left with the three points. Marc Overmars' goal in the 79th minute stunned the majority of the 55,174 into silence. The diminutive Dutch winger had been a constant menace to United's defence throughout and he outpaced Gary Neville to slot home under Schmeichel after Patrick Vieira had headed the ball into his path. And for the first time in weeks, the Premiership title was no longer in the hands of the champions. 'We're now looking to win seven league matches in a row which is what we're capable of doing if we get key players back,' said Alex Ferguson afterwards.

ALLSPORT

Bergkamp keeps his eyes on the prize as Man United crash at home

Leeds United put in their most impressive performance of the season to date with a stunning 5–0 victory against Derby at Pride Park on 15 March. It was the first time the Rams had conceded more than two goals at their new stadium and George Graham's men cut Derby's defence to shreds with a fine counter-attacking performance. Leeds were 3–0 to the good by half-time with goals from Gunnar Halle, Lee Bowyer and an own-goal from Derby defender Jacob Larsen. Kewell and Hasselbaink converted smartly after the interval to leave their delighted manager singing the praises of his team. 'We played some great football with a lot of style,' said Graham after the game.

Gunnar Halle looks on as Leeds slot another in their 5–0 demolition of Derby at Pride Park

ALLSPORT

Monday May 17 1999

Tuesday May 18 1999

Wednesday May 19 1999

Thursday May 20 1999

Friday May 21 1999

Saturday May 22 1999
FA Cup Final

Sunday May 23 1999

Monday May 24 1999

Tuesday May 25 1999

Wednesday May 26 1999

Thursday May 27 1999

Friday May 28 1999

Saturday May 29 1999

Sunday May 30 1999

On 17 March Alan Kelly pulled off three spectacular saves in a tense penalty shootout against Coventry City to send Sheffield United into the semi-finals of the FA Cup. Republic of Ireland keeper Kelly saved spot-kicks from Dion Dublin, David Burrows and Simon Hayworth, but it was the Blades who were grateful that the game went into extra time. Coventry's Paul Telfer opened the scoring in the 10th minute as Gordon Strachan's men dominated the first half hour. United pressed for an equaliser, but they had to wait until the 89th minute, when the Sky Blues failed to clear a corner and skipper David Holdsworth banged in a volley from 12 yards.

ALLSPORT

Darren Huckerby does his best to get Coventry to Wembley

Arsenal defeated London neighbours West Ham in a dramatic penalty shootout to send the Gunners through to an FA Cup semi-final meeting with Wolves. Tony Adams' spot-kick settled the issue, but Arsenal had to play over half the game without PFA Player of the Year Dennis Bergkamp. The Dutch striker was sent off by referee Mike Reed after he elbowed Hammers skipper Steve Lomas, Bergkamp's second dismissal of the season. Nicolas Anelka struck at the end of the first period to give Arsenal the lead before former Gunners' striker John Hartson equalised six minutes from the end. Five spot-kicks were missed in the penalty shootout but Tony Adams kept his nerve to fire past Bernard Lamas. It was a bad week for Arsenal's Premiership rivals Manchester United who crashed out of the European Cup to Monaco.

London derbies are rarely quiet affairs. Neither Ray Parlour nor John Moncur are about to change that

ALLSPORT

ALLSPORT

According to Barnsley, the referee hadn't learned the script properly, but the players certainly acted their parts in a resoundingly good argument

Referee Gary Willard sent off three Barnsley players in an explosive encounter against Liverpool at Oakwell on 28 March. At one stage, the proceedings became so heated that the Worthing official and his assistants had to leave the field with a police escort after irate Barnsley fans ran onto the pitch. A brace each from Barnsley skipper Neil Redfearn and Karl-Heinz Riedle suggested that the teams would share the spoils, only for Steve MacManaman to slot home from close range in the final minute to give Liverpool three points. However, it was the sendings off that made the headlines. 'The referee lost the plot, it's as simple as that,' said irate Barnsley boss Danny Wilson.

Chelsea player-manager Gianluca Vialli left himself out of his Coca-Cola Cup Final squad but ended up lifting the trophy. Two goals in extra time broke the stalemate and left Bryan Robson's Middlesbrough bridesmaids yet again. It was Boro's third Wembley defeat in 12 months. But it was a great day for Vialli, who preferred Mark Hughes and Tore Andre Flo to himself, and the victory came only weeks after the sensational departure of Ruud Gullit. Frank Sinclair opened the scoring in the first half of extra time before Roberto Di Matteo settled the issue. And Paul Gascoigne's Middlesbrough debut could easily have ended with his sending off. He was booked for a scything challenge on Zola and later made bad tackles on Hughes and Wise.

Quiz 6 About the Premier League

1 Which of the following clubs has not won the Premiership?

a) Liverpool
b) Blackburn Rovers
c) Leeds United

2 Who finished bottom of the Premiership after the 1996-97 season?

a) Nottingham Forest
b) Middlesbrough
c) Sunderland

3 Who was Young Player of the Year in 1994?

a) Andy Cole
b) David Beckham
c) Robbie Fowler

It could have been Ruud's, but Vialli's happy with the Coca-Cola Cup

ALLSPORT

4 Who has scored the fastest hat-trick in Premiership history?

a) Dion Dublin
b) Robbie Fowler
c) Alan Shearer

5 Which was the first ever Premiership season?

a) 1990-91
b) 1991-92
c) 1992-93

6 What was the first Premiership game to be broadcast on satellite television?

a) Nottingham Forest v Liverpool
b) Arsenal v Manchester United
c) Tottenham v Chelsea

7 Which club holds the record for the number of goals conceded in a Premiership season?

a) Swindon Town
b) Middlesbrough
c) Nottingham Forest

8 Which two clubs share the record for the fewest number of goals conceded in a Premiership season?

a) Arsenal and Leeds United
b) Arsenal and Blackburn Rovers
c) Arsenal and Manchester United

9 Which of the following Premiership clubs was not a member of the original Football League?

a) Manchester United
b) Aston Villa
c) Everton

10 Who was the 1992 Manager of the Year?

a) Kenny Dalglish
b) George Graham
c) Howard Wilkinson

Answers: 1.a 2.b 3.a 4.b 5.c 6.a 7.a 8.c 9.a 10.c

Monday May 31 1999

Tuesday June 1 1999

Wednesday June 2 1999

Thursday June 3 1999

Friday June 4 1999

Saturday June 5 1999

Sunday June 6 1999

Monday June 7 1999

Tuesday June 8 1999

Wednesday June 9 1999

Thursday June 10 1999

Friday June 11 1999

Saturday June 12 1999

Sunday June 13 1999

On 5 April, Newcastle United put their torrid season to one side to reach their first FA Cup Final for 24 years. A second-half strike by Alan Shearer, who was three years old last time the Magpies played in a Wembley final, settled the issue. The England striker's downward header was saved by Alan Kelly, but Shearer followed it up to strike home. Newcastle largely dominated proceedings but had keeper Shay Given to thank for two excellent late saves to ensure their progression. 'They've got quality players and after the first half, when they hit the post and had a couple kicked off the line, I knew it would be hard,' said Blades boss Steve Thompson.

ALLSPORT

Gary Speed aims to take Newcastle to Wembley, the first time in 24 years

'We did not deserve anything here. Barnsley showed a lot more spirit than us.' That was Ron Atkinson's verdict after his Sheffield Wednesday side slumped to a derby defeat against Tyke rivals Barnsley on 11 April. And it was a loss which edged the Owls ever closer to the drop-zone, just weeks after they looked safe for a mid-table berth. Ashley Ward opened the scoring, poking home from close range in the second half. Substitute Jan Fjortoft struck seven minutes later to guarantee Barnsley the three points, giving them a faint chance of beating the drop.

Even Guy Whittingham couldn't stop Barnsley rolling their neighbours in their encounter

ALLSPORT

Monday June 14 1999

Tuesday June 15 1999

Wednesday June 16 1999

Thursday June 17 1999

Friday June 18 1999

Saturday June 19 1999

Sunday June 20 1999

Monday June 21 1999

Tuesday June 22 1999

Wednesday June 23 1999

Thursday June 24 1999

Friday June 25 1999

Saturday June 26 1999

Sunday June 27 1999

25 April: Tottenham Hotspur won the crucial battle against relegation rivals Newcastle, with goals from frontmen Jürgen Klinsmann and Les Ferdinand. But the best performance of the day came from Spurs' midfielder David Ginola, who ran the Newcastle defence ragged all afternoon. The former Newcastle winger set up the first, when he turned neatly past Warren Barton on the right and his curling cross was met by the head of Klinsmann. And in the second half, Les Ferdinand nodded home a Ginola corner to give Spurs three vital points. Christian Gross was delighted with Ferdinand's return after injury: 'This was his best performance for me. He wants to save Spurs and go to the World Cup,' said Gross.

ALLSPORT

Running Newcastle ragged – the Klinsmann (& Ferdinand) show

Brave Barnsley's year in the Premiership ended in relegation at Leicester City on 2 May. The Tykes produced yet another battling performance at Filbert Street but fell to a second half goal from Theo Zagorakis, which proved enough to give Martin O'Neill's men an outside chance of European qualification. Barnsley did create opportunities but both Ashley Ward and Jan Aage Fjortoft were denied by Kasey Keller in the Leicester goal. Despite relegation, Tykes' boss Danny Wilson remained relatively upbeat. 'It was not just today's game but our performances throughout the season which have caused us to be relegated,' he said. But he add: 'In the second half of the season my players have been a credit to themselves – and me.'

Premiership survival or European glory? Barnsley and Leicester battle for two prizes

Allsport

Monday June 28 1999

Tuesday June 29 1999

Wednesday June 30 1999

Thursday July 1 1999

Friday July 2 1999

Saturday July 3 1999

Sunday July 4 1999

ALLSPORT

Phew! A bit close, but at least there's another year for Everton to pull back from the brink

Arsenal were crowned champions for the first time since 1991, sealing the Premiership title with a 4–0 win over Everton at Highbury on 3 May. The Gunners got off to a great start when Emmanuel Petit's free kick was headed into his own net by Everton defender Slaven Bilic after just six minutes. Dutch winger Marc Overmars netted a brace to make the game safe before Tony Adams ran onto Steve Bould's through ball to finish superbly in the 89th minute. Arsene Wenger, the first foreign coach to a lead a side to the championship, was delighted. 'I always thought we could do it and everybody here has contributed to our success. We played like champions,' said Wenger. Arsenal skipper Tony Adams was delighted, too. 'I am determined to savour every moment. I don't remember too much from last time but I will this time.' he said.

Bolton Wanderers' brave fight for Premiership survival ended in failure at Stamford Bridge on 10 May. Colin Todd's men slipped through the trap door after a 2–0 defeat by Chelsea, but it was a cruel way to go down. Rivals Everton only survived because they conceded five fewer goals than Wanderers. Per Frandson had a first-half effort cleared off the line by Dennis Wise before Blues' player-boss Gianluca Vialli scored 15 minutes from time. And Jody Morris added a second near the death to send Bolton crashing. 'We came close to a great escape but I just couldn't manage it,' said a heartbroken Colin Todd afterwards. 'I feel sorry for the players and for our supporters.'

Everton survived relegation by the skin of their teeth, but after Dion Dublin equalised Gareth Farrelly's opener, the Goodison Park faithful had to endure a nail-biting finish. As it was, Farrelly's early strike – his first league goal since a summer switch from Aston Villa – has ensured Everton's start in the top league in the 199899 campaign, their 45th consecutive season. Nick Barmby should have made Everton safe in the 84th minute when Danny Cadamarteri was upended by Paul Williams, but the former Spurs striker's spot kick was saved by Hedman. Howard Kendall was a relieved man: 'This was a day I would not want to go through again and we won't as long as I am manager,' he said. Hmmm...

And that was 1997-98. Tony Adams and Arsene Wenger were ready for the FA Cup too

ALLSPORT

1998/99 PROGRESS CHART FOR SUPPORTERS OF

		DATE	SCORE	POINTS	PLACE	REFEREE
Aston Villa ....v.................. Arsenal	HOME	/ /	–			
	AWAY	/ /	–			
Aston Villa ....v .... Blackburn Rovers	HOME	/ /	–			
	AWAY	/ /	–			
Aston Villa ....v......... Charlton Athletic	HOME	/ /	–			
	AWAY	/ /	–			
Aston Villa ....v.................. Chelsea	HOME	/ /	–			
	AWAY	/ /	–			
Aston Villa ....v............ Coventry City	HOME	/ /	–			
	AWAY	/ /	–			
Aston Villa ....v............ Derby County	HOME	/ /	–			
	AWAY	/ /	–			
Aston Villa ....v.................. Everton	HOME	/ /	–			
	AWAY	/ /	–			
Aston Villa ....v .... Leeds United	HOME	/ /	–			
	AWAY	/ /	–			
Aston Villa ....v............ Leicester City	HOME	/ /	–			
	AWAY	/ /	–			
Aston Villa ....v................. Liverpool	HOME	/ /	–			
	AWAY	/ /	–			
Aston Villa ....v....... Manchester United	HOME	/ /	–			
	AWAY	/ /	–			
Aston Villa ....v .... Middlesbrough	HOME	/ /	–			
	AWAY	/ /	–			
Aston Villa ....v .... Newcastle United	HOME	/ /	–			
	AWAY	/ /	–			
Aston Villa ....v .... Nottingham Forest	HOME	/ /	–			
	AWAY	/ /	–			
Aston Villa ....v ..... Sheffield Wednesday	HOME	/ /	–			
	AWAY	/ /	–			
Aston Villa ....v............ Southampton	HOME	/ /	–			
	AWAY	/ /	–			
Aston Villa ....v....... Tottenham Hotspur	HOME	/ /	–			
	AWAY	/ /	–			
Aston Villa ....v......... West Ham United	HOME	/ /	–			
	AWAY	/ /	–			
Aston Villa ....v............... Wimbledon	HOME	/ /	–			
	AWAY	/ /	–			

MATCH NOTES

	GOALSCORERS	YELLOW CARDS	RED CARDS	COMMENTS

MATCH NOTES

SUPPORTERS' AWAY INFORMATION

UNITED KINGDOM AIRPORTS

Aberdeen (Dyce)	01224 722331
Belfast (Aldegrove)	01849 422888
Birmingham International	0121 767-5511
Blackpool	01253 343434
Bournemouth (Hurn)	01202 593939
Bristol (Luisgate)	01275 474444
Cambridge	01223 61133
Cardiff	01446 711211
East Midlands	01332 852852
Edinburgh	0131333-1000
Glasgow	0141 887 1111
Humberside	01652 688491
Inverness (Dalcross)	01463 232471
Leeds & Bradford (Yeadon)	01132 509696
Liverpool (Speke)	0151 486-8877
London (Gatwick)	01293 535353
London (Heathrow)	0181 759-4321
London (London City)	0171 474-5555
London (Stanstead)	01279 680500
Luton	01582 405100
Lydd	01797 320401
Manchester (Ringway)	0161 489-3000
Newcastle (Woolsington)	0191 286-0966
Newquay (St. Mawgan)	01637 860551
Norwich	01603 411923
Plymouth	01752 772752
Prestwick	01292 479822
Southampton	01703 629600
Southend	01702 340201
Stornoway	01851 702256
Teesside (Darlington)	01325 332811
Westland Heliport	0171 228-0181

PASSPORT OFFICES

London 0171 799-2728
Clive House, 70–78 Petty France, SW1H 9HD

Liverpool 0151 237-3010
5th Floor, India Buildings, Water Street, L2 0QZ

Peterborough 01733 555688
UK Passport Agency, Aragon Court, Northminster Road, Peterborough PE1 1QG

Glasgow 0141 332-4441
3 Northgate, 96 Milton Street, Cowcadens, Glasgow G4 0BT

Newport 01633 473700
Olympia House, Upper Dock Street, Newport, Gwent NP9 1XQ

Belfast 01232 330214
Hampton House, 47–53 High Street, Belfast BT1 2QS

TOURIST & TRAVEL INFORMATION CENTRES

ENGLAND

Birmingham (NEC)	0121 780-4321
Blackpool	01253 21623
Bournemouth	01202 789789
Brighton	01273 323755
Cambridge	01223 322640
Chester	01244 351609
Colchester	01206 282920
Dover	01304 205108
Durham	0191 384-3720
Hull	01482 223559
Lancaster	01524 32878
Leicester	01162 650555
Lincoln	01522 529828
Liverpool	0151 708-8838
Manchester	0161 234-3157
Newcastle-upon-Tyne	0191 261-0691
Newquay	01603 871345
Norwich	01603 666071
Oxford	01865 726871
Portsmouth	01705 826722
Southampton	01703 221106
Torquay	01803 297428
York	01904 620557

SCOTLAND

Aberdeen	01224 632727
Edinburgh	0131 557-1700
Glasgow	0141 848-4440
Stirling	01786 475019

WALES

Cardiff	01222 227281
Wrexham	01978 292015

MAIN INTER-CITY RAIL CONNECTIONS FOR
ENGLAND & WALES

FERRY SERVICES

B&I Line	Liverpool	0151 2273131
Brittany Ferries	Plymouth	01752 221321
Color Line	Newcastle	0191 2961313
Hoverspeed	Dover	01304 240241
North Sea Ferries	Hull	01482 795141
Olau Line	Sheerness	01795 666666
P&O European	Dover	01304 203388
P&O Scottish	Aberdeen	01224 589111
Scandinavian	Harwich	01255 240240
Stena Sealink	Ashford	01233 647047
Swansea Cork	Swansea	01792 456116

TRAIN OPERATOR CONTACTS

See following page

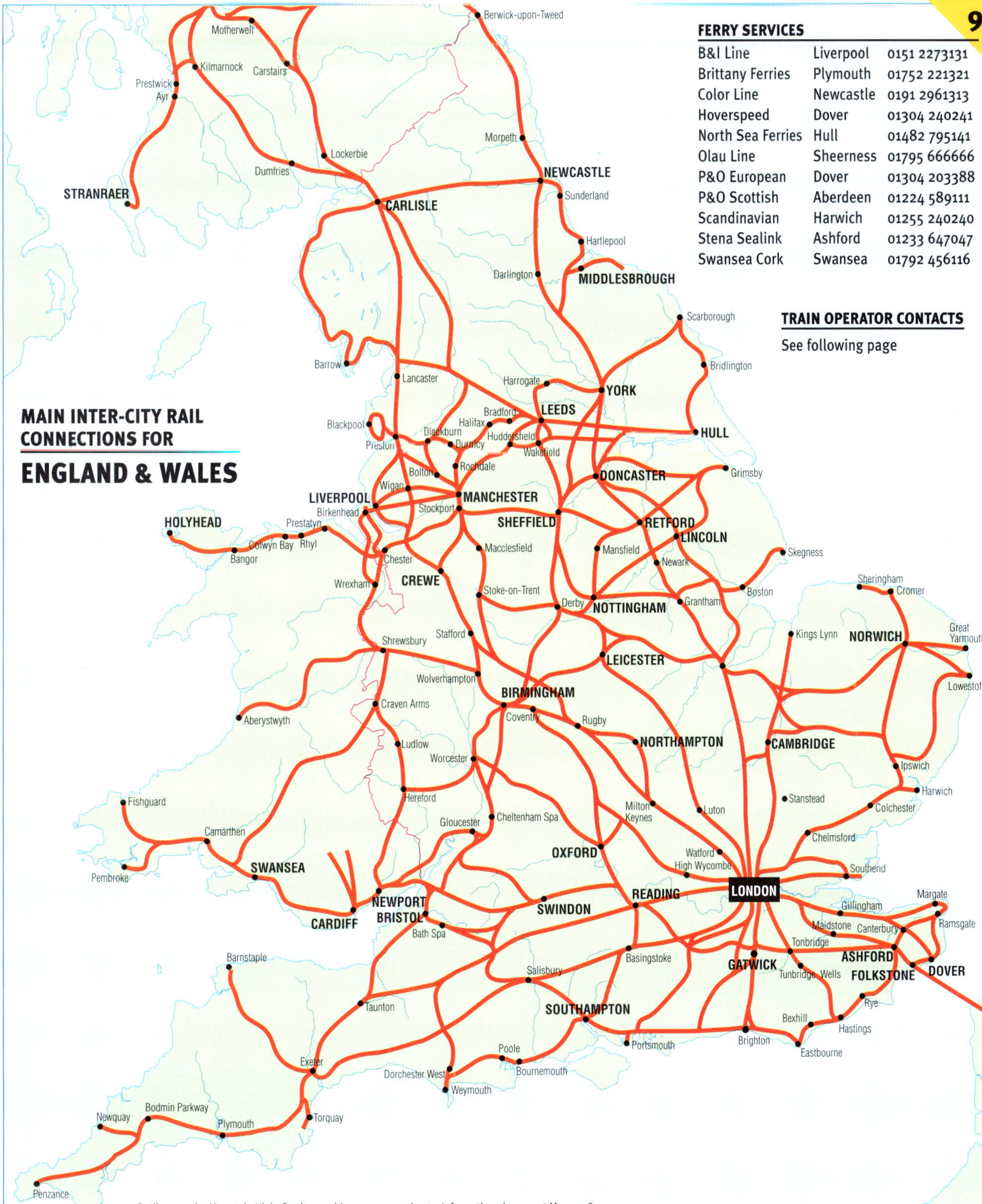

Outline map by Mountain High. Station positions are approximate. Information given as at May 1998

SUPPORTERS' AWAY INFORMATION

TRAIN OPERATORS

ANGLIA RAILWAYS
15-25 Artillery Lane, London, E1 7HA
Tel 01473 693333
Fax 01473 693497

CARDIFF RAILWAY CO
10th Floor, Brunel House, 2 Fitzalan Rd,
Cardiff CF2 1SA
Tel 01222 430000
Fax 01222 480463

CENTRAL TRAINS
PO Box 4323, Stanier House, 10 Holliday Street
Birmingham B1 1TH
Tel 0121 654 4444
Fax 0121 654 4461

CHILTERN RAILWAY CO
Western House, 14 Rickfords Hill, Aylesbury
HP20 2RX
Tel 01296 332100
Fax 01296 332126

CONNEX SOUTH CENTRAL
Stephenson House, 2 Cherry Orchard Road,
Croydon CR9 6JB
Tel 0181 667 2780
Fax 0181 667 2906

EUROSTAR (UK)
Eurostar House, Waterloo Station, London
SE1 8SE
Tel 0171 928 5151

GATWICK EXPRESS
52 Grosvenor Gardens, London SW1W OAU
Tel 0171 973 5005
Fax 0171 973 5038

GREAT EASTERN RAILWAY
Hamilton House, 3 Appold Street, London
EC2A 2AA
Tel 0645 50 50 00
Fax 01473 693745

GREAT NORTH EATERN RAILWAY
Main Headquarters Building, York YO1 1HT
Tel 01904 653022
Fax 01904 523392

GREAT WESTERN TRAINS CO
Milford House, 1 Milton Street, Swindon SN1 1HL
Tel 01793 499400
Fax 01793 499460

HEATHROW EXPRESS
4th Floor, Cardinal Point, Newall Rd, Hounslow
Middlesex TW6 2QS
Tel 0181 745 0578
Fax 0181 745 1627

ISLAND LINE
Ryde St Johns Road Station, Ryde, Isle Of Wight
PO33 2BA
Tel 01983 812591
Fax 01983 817879

LTS RAIL
Central House, Clifftown Road, Southend-on-Sea
SS1 1AB
Tel 01702 357889

MERSEYRAIL ELECTRICS
Rail House, Lord Nelson Street, Liverpool L1 1JF
Tel 0151 709 8292
Fax 0151 702 2413

MIDLAND MAINLINE
Midland House, Nelson Street, Derby,
East Midlands DE1 2SA
Tel 0345 221125
Fax 01332 262011

NORTH WESTERN TRAINS
PO Box 44, Rail House, Store Street
Manchester M60 1DQ
Tel 0161 228 2141
Fax 0161 228 5003

REGIONAL RAILWAYS NORTH EAST
Main Headquarters Building, York YO1 1HT
Tel 01904 653022

SCOTRAIL RAILWAYS
Caledonian Chambers, 87 Union Street
Glasgow G1 3TA
Tel 0141 332 9811

SILVERLINK TRAIN SERVICES
65-67 Clarendon Raod, Watford WD1 1DP
Tel 01923 207258
Fax 01923 207023

SOUTH WEST TRAINS
Friars Bridge Court, 41-45 Blackfrairs Road
London SE1 8NZ
Tel 0171 928 5151
Fax 0171 902 3208

THAMESLINK RAIL
Friars Bridge, 41-45 Blackfriars Road,
London SE1 8NZ
Tel 0171 620 5760
Fax 0171 620 5099

THAMES TRAINS
Venture House, 37 Blagrave Street, Reading
RG1 1PZ
Tel 0118 908 3678
Fax 0118 957 9006

VIRGIN TRAINS
85 Smallbrook Queensway, Birmingham B5 4HA
Tel 0121 654 7400
Fax 0121 654 7487

WALES & WEST
Brunel House, 2 Fitzalan Rd, Cardiff CF2 1SU
Tel 01222 430400
Fax 01222 430214

WEST ANGLIA GREAT NORTHERN RAILWAY
Hertford House, 1 Cranwood Street, London
EC1V 9GT
Tel 0345 818919
Fax 01223 453606

WEST COAST RAILWAY COMPANY
Warton Road, Carnforth, Lancashire LA5 9HX
Tel 01524 732100
Fax 01524 735518

SOCCER RELATED INTERNET BOOKMARKS

The following three pages are a listing of soccer websites, some of which you may find useful to bookmark. As any internet browser will know all too well, URLs change, move or become obsolete at the drop of a hat. At the time of going to press all the ones listed were active.

If you are new to internet browsing, the following information on entering the URL addresses should be observed. Because of the way the address lines are printed, those longer than the width of the column are broken into two lines, the second slightly indented. Nevertheless, all the characters of the address should be typed in as one line, with no spaces between characters. If your edition or version of browser already enters the 'http://' characters, or does not require them, omit these from the URL address.

Where sites are official, it states so in brackets after the site name. Any useful notes about the site are given after the name in square brackets.

WORLD CUP RELATED PAGES

Football Web in Japan
http://www.nidnet.com/link/socweb.html
CBS SportsLine - Soccer
http://www.sportsline.com/u/soccer/index.html
Teams of the World
http://www.islandia.is/totw/
World Cup - Soccernet
http://www.soccernet.com/u/soccer/worldcup98/index.html
World Cup 1998 - CBS SportsLine
http://www.sportsline.com/u/soccer/worldcup98/qualifying/index.html
World Cup Soccer - France 98 - Coupe du Monde
http://www.worldcup.com/english/index.html

FOOTBALL RELATED

1997 edition of the Laws of the Game
http://www.fifa.com/fifa/handbook/laws/index.laws.html
Soccer Books [good reference]
http://www.soccer-books.co.uk
British Society of Sports History [reference material]
http://www.umist.ac.uk/UMIST_Sport/bssh.html
Buchanan Brigade Messge Bd Thirty-Three
http://www.buchanan.org/mb33.html
Communicata Football
http://www.communicata.co.uk/lookover/football/
Division 1 Web Pages [relates to the Nationwide leagues]
http://www.users.globalnet.co.uk/~emmas/ndiv1.htm
Division 2 Web Pages [old Endsleigh rather than the Nationwide]
http://www.uwm.edu/People/dyce/htfc/clubs/div2-www.html
England [Engerland]
http://www.users.dircon.co.uk/~england/england/
England [Green Flags England team pages]
http://www.greenflag.co.uk/te/fslist.html
England [English Soccernet - National Team - News]
http://www.soccernet.com/english/national/news/index.html
England
http://www.englandfc.com/
English Club Homepages
http://pluto.webbernet.net/~bob/engclub.html
FAI - Irish International
http://www.fai.ie/
GeordieSport!
http://www.geordiepride.demon.co.uk/geordiesport.htm
L & M Referees' Society - Soccer Pages
http://www.lancs.ac.uk/ug/williams/soccer.htm
Northern Ireland [Norn Iron!: The NI International Football 'zine]
http://students.un.umist.ac.uk/gbh/index.html
Notts Association
http://www.innotts.co.uk/~soccerstats/gallery/nmf8.htm
Scotland [Rampant Scotland - Sport]
http://scotland.rampant.com/sport.htm
Scotland
http://web.city.ac.uk/~sh393/euro/scotland.htm
Scottish Football Association (Official)
http://www.scottishfa.co.uk/
Scottish Mailing Lists
http://www.isfa.com/isfa/lists/scotland.htm
Simply the Best
http://www.int-foot-fame.com/famers1.htm
Soccer ScoreSheet History List
http://www.kazmax.demon.co.uk/websheet/tm000309.htm
Soccer-Tables
http://www.marwin.ch/sport/fb/index.e.html
SoccerSearch: Players:G-P
http://www.soccersearch.com/Players/G-P/
SoccerSpace, Football & Soccer Links
http://www.winbet.sci.fi/soccerspace/links.htm
Team England - Fixtures & Results
http://ourworld.compuserve.com/homepages/nic_king/england/fixtures.htm
The Association of Football Statisticians
http://www.innotts.co.uk/~soccerstats/
The Aylesbury Branch of the Referees Association
http://homepages.bucks.net/~bigmick/
The Daily Soccer
http://www.dailysoccer.com/
The Football Supporters' Association (FSA)
http://www.fsa.org.uk/
US Soccer History Archives
http://www.sover.net/~spectrum/index.html
Welsh Football,Football wales,faw,welsh fa,ryan giggs
http://www.citypages.co.uk/faw/

ENGLISH PREMIERSHIP

Arsenal
http://www.arsenal.co.uk/
Aston Villa
http://www.geocities.com/Colosseum/Field/6089/
Aston Villa
http://www.villan.demon.co.uk/
Aston Villa
http://www.gbar.dtu.dk/~c937079/AVFC/index.html
Aston Villa (Official)
http://www.gbar.dtu.dk/~c937079/CB/
Barnsley
http://www.geocities.com/Colosseum/Field/6059/bfc.html
Barnsley
http://www.u-net.com/westex/bfc.htm
Barnsley
http://www.radders.skynet.co.uk/
Barnsley
http://upload.virgin.net/d.penty/Copacabarnsley/Copacabarnsley.htm
Barnsley
http://members.aol.com/JLister/bfc/bfc.htm
Blackburn Rovers
http://www.brfc-supporters.org.uk/
Blackburn Rovers (Official)
http://www.rovers.co.uk/
Bolton Wanderers
http://www.hankins.demon.co.uk/bwscl/index.html
Bolton Wanderers
http://www.netcomuk.co.uk/~cjw/football.html
Bolton Wanderers
http://www.geocities.com/Colosseum/4433/
Bolton Wanderers
http://mail.freeway.co.uk/druid/
Bolton Wanderers (Official)
http://www.boltonwfc.co.uk/
Charlton Athletic
http://www.demon.co.uk/casc/index.html
Chelsea
http://www.geocities.com/Colosseum/1457/chelsea.html
Chelsea
http://web.ukonline.co.uk/Members/jf.lettice/cfcmain.html
Chelsea
http://www.jack.dircon.net/chelsea/
Chelsea
http://fans-of.chelsea-fc.com/csr/
Chelsea FC (Official)
http://www.chelseafc.co.uk/chelsea/frontpage.shtml
Coventry City [mpegs of goals... that's it]
http://karpaty.tor.soliton.com/ccfcgoals/
Coventry City [The Sky Blue Superplex]
http://www.geocities.com/TimesSquare/Dungeon/1641/page4.html
Coventry City
http://www.warwick.ac.uk/~cudbu/SkyBlues.html
Coventry City (Official)
http://www.ccfc.co.uk/
Derby County
http://lard.sel.cam.ac.uk/derby_county/
Derby County
http://www.cheme.cornell.edu/~jwillits/this.html
Derby County
http://easyweb.easynet.co.uk/~nickwheat/ramsnet.html
Derby County
http://home.sol.no/~einasand/derby.htm
Derby County
http://www.cheme.cornell.edu/~jwillits/derby2.html#History
Derby County
http://www.derby-county.com/main.htm
Derby County (Official)
http://www.dcfc.co.uk/dcfc/index.html
Everton FC (Official)
http://www.connect.org.uk/everton/
Leeds United
http://www.lufc.co.uk/
Leeds United
http://spectrum.tcns.co.uk/cedar/leeds.htm
Leeds United
http://www.csc.liv.ac.uk/users/tim/Leeds/
Leeds United (Official - CarlingNet)
http://www.fa-premier.com/club/lufc/
Leicester City (Official)
http://www.lcfc.co.uk/141097b.htm
Liverpool
http://akureyri.ismennt.is/~jongeir/
Liverpool
http://www.soccernet.com/livrpool/
Liverpool
http://www.connect.org.uk/anfield/
Manchester United
http://www.cs.indiana.edu/hyplan/ccheah/posts.html
Manchester United
http://www.geocities.com/SouthBeach/6367/index.html
Manchester United
http://www.sky.co.uk/sports/manu/
Manchester United
http://www.cybernet.dk/users/barrystorv/
Manchester United
http://home.pacific.net.sg/~jerping/
Manchester United
http://sunhehi.phy.uic.edu/~clive/MUFC/home.html
Manchester United
http://www.iol.ie/~mmurphy/red_devils/mufc.htm
Manchester United
http://www.davewest.demon.co.uk/
Manchester United
http://www.webcom.com/~solution/mufc/manu.html
Manchester United
http://ourworld.compuserve.com/homepages/red_devil/
Manchester United
http://xanadu.centrum.is/~runarhi/
Manchester United
http://web.city.ac.uk/~sh393/mufc.htm
Manchester United
http://www.wsu.edu:8080/~mmarks/Giggs.html
Manchester United
http://osiris.sunderland.ac.uk/online/access/manutd/redshome.html
Manchester United
http://www.u-net.com/~pitman/
Manchester United
http://www.geocities.com/Colosseum/2483/
Manchester United
http://www.wsu.edu:8080/~mmarks/mufclinks.html
Manchester United
http://gladstone.uoregon.edu:80/~jsetzen/mufc.html
Manchester United
http://members.hknet.com/~siukin/
Newcastle United
http://www.swan.co.uk/TOTT
Newcastle United
http://www.nufc.com
Newcastle United
http://www.btinternet.com/~the.magpie/history1.htm
Newcastle United
http://www.ccacyber.com/nufc/
Newcastle United
http://sunflower.singnet.com.sg/~resa21/
Nottingham Forest
http://users.homenet.ie/~aidanhut/
Nottingham Forest
http://www.thrustworld.co.uk/users/kryten/forest/
Nottingham Forest
http://hem1.passagen.se/pearce/index.htm
Nottingham Forest
http://www.innotts.co.uk/~joe90/forest.htm
Nottingham Forest
http://ourworld.compuserve.com/homepages/kencrossland/
Nottingham Forest (Official)
http://www.nottingham-forest.co.uk/frames.html
Sheffield Wednesday
http://www.crg.cs.nott.ac.uk/Users/anb/Football/stats/swfcarch.htm
Sheffield Wednesday
http://www.rhi.hi.is/~jbj/sheffwed/opnun.htm

BOOKMARKS

Sheffield Wednesday
http://www.geocities.com/Colosseum/2938/
Sheffield Wednesday
http://www.cs.nott.ac.uk/~anb/Football/
Southampton [Saintsweb]
http://www.soton.ac.uk/~saints/
Southampton [Marching In]
http://www.saintsfans.com/marchingin/
Tottenham Hotspur [White Hart Site]
http://www.xpress.se/~ssab0019/webring/index.html
Tottenham Hotspur [Felix Gills' Page]
http://www.gilnet.demon.co.uk/spurs.htm
Tottenham Hotspur
http://www.personal.u-net.com/~spurs/
Tottenham Hotspur [check Spurs results year-by-year - just stats]
http://www.bobexcell.demon.co.uk/
Tottenham Hotspur
http://www.btinternet.com/~matt.cook/
Tottenham Hotspur (Official)
http://www.spurs.co.uk/welcome.html
West Ham United
http://www.ecs.soton.ac.uk/saints/premier/westham.htm
West Ham United
http://www.westhamunited.co.uk/
Wimbledon
http://www.fa-premier.com/cgi-bin/fetch/club/wfc/home.html?team='WIM'
Wimbledon [unofficial - WISA]
http://www.wisa.org.uk/
Wimbledon [Womble.Net - Independent Wimbledon FC Internet 'zine]
http://www.geocities.com/SunsetStrip/Studio/6112/womblnet.html
Wimbledon [very basic]
http://www.aracnet.com/~davej/football.htm
Wimbledon [unofficial - USA]
http://soyokaze.biosci.ohio-state.edu/~dcp/wimbledon/womble.html
Wimbledon
http://www.city.ac.uk/~sh393/prem/wimbeldon.htm
Wimbledon
http://www.netkonect.co.uk/b/brenford/wimbledon/
Wimbledon [unofficial - WISA]
http://www.soi.city.ac.uk/homes/ec564/donswisa.html
Wimbledon [John's Wimbledon FC page]
http://www.soi.city.ac.uk/homes/ec564/dons.top.html
Wimbledon (Official)
http://www.wimbledon-fc.co.uk/

ENGLISH DIVISION 1

Birmingham City [PlanetBlues]
http://www.isfa.com/server/web/planetblues/
Birmingham City [BCFC Supports Club Redditch Branch]
http://www.fortunecity.com/olympia/ovett/135/
Birmingham City [Richy's B'ham City Page]
http://www.rshill.demon.co.uk/blues.htm
Bradford City
http://www.legend.co.uk/citygent/index.html
Bury
http://www.brad.ac.uk/%7edjmartin/bury1.html
Crystal Palace
http://www.gold.net/users/az21/cp_home.htm
Fulham [The Independent Fulham Fans Website: History]
http://www.fulhamfc.co.uk/History/history.html
Fulham [FulhamWeb]
http://www.btinternet.com/~aredfern/
Fulham [Black & White Pages]
http://www.wilf.demon.co.uk/fulhamfc/ffc.html
Fulham [unofficial - The Fulham Football Club Mailing List]
http://www.users.dircon.co.uk/~troyj/fulham/
Fulham
http://zeus.bris.ac.uk/~chmsl/fulham/fulham.html
Fulham
http://www.netlondon.com/cgi-local/wilma/spo.873399737.html
Fulham (Official) [mostly merchandising]
http://www.fulham-fc.co.uk/
Huddersfield Town
http://www.geocities.com/Colosseum/4401/index.html
Huddersfield Town
http://ftp.csd.uwm.edu/People/dyce/htfc/
Huddersfield Town
http://granby.nott.ac.uk/~ppykara/htfc/
Huddersfield Town
http://www.uwm.edu:80/~dyce/htfc/index.html
Ipswich Town [MATCHfacts - Datafile]
http://www.matchfacts.com/mfdclub/ipswich.htm
Ipswich Town
http://www.sys.uea.ac.uk/Recreation/Sport/itfc/
Ipswich Town [Those Were The Days]
http://www.twtd.co.uk/
Ipswich Town
http://members.wbs.net/homepages/a/d/a/adamcable.html
Ipswich Town [The Online Portman Vista]
http://www.btinternet.com/~bluearmy/index2.html
Ipswich Town [unofficial - Latest News - not really]
http://www.rangey.demon.co.uk/ipswich.htm
Ipswich Town [IPSWICH TOWN tribute]
http://www.geocities.com/Colosseum/Track/5399/
Ipswich Town [The Ipswich Town VRML Site - techy, not much else]
http://www.sys.uea.ac.uk/Recreation/Sport/itfc/vrml/vrml.html
Ipswich Town
http://homepages.enterprise.net/meo/itfc2.html
Ipswich Town (Official)
http://www.itfc.co.uk/
Manchester City
http://www.uit.no/mancity/
Manchester City (Official)
http://www.mcfc.co.uk/
Middlesbrough
http://www.hk.super.net/~tllovd/personal/boro.html
Norwich City
http://ncfc.netcom.co.uk/ncfc/
Oxford United
http://www.aligrafix.co.uk/ag/fun/home/OxTales/default.html
Oxford United
http://www.netlink.co.uk//users/oufc1/index.html
Port Vale
http://www.netcentral.co.uk/~iglover/index.html
Port Vale
http://web.dcs.hull.ac.uk/people/pjp/PortVale/PortVale.html
Portsmouth [unofficial - History]
http://www.mech.port.ac.uk/StaffP/pb/history.html
Portsmouth [Links page]
http://www.imsport.co.uk/imsport/ims/tt/035/club.html
Queens Park Rangers
http://www-dept.cs.ucl.ac.uk/students/M.Pemble/index.html
Reading
http://www.i-way.co.uk/~readingfc/
Sheffield United
http://www.shef.ac.uk/city/blades/
Sheffield United
http://pine.shu.ac.uk/~cmssa/bifa.html
Sheffield United (Official)
http://www.sufc.co.uk/
Stoke City
http://www.cs.bham.ac.uk/~jdr/scfc/scfc.htm
Sunderland (Official)
http://www.sunderland-afc.com/
Swindon Town
http://www.bath.ac.uk/~ee3cmk/swindon/home.html
Tranmere Rovers
http://www.connect.org.uk/merseyworld/tarantula/
Tranmere Rovers
http://www.brad.ac.uk/~mjhesp/tran.htm
West Bromwich Albion
http://pages.prodigy.com/FL/baggie/
West Bromwich Albion
http://www.gold.net/users/cp78/
West Bromwich Albion - Official
http://www.wba.co.uk/
Wolverhampton Wanderers [The Wandering Wolf]
http://www.angelfire.com/wv/Quants/index.html
Wolverhampton Wanderers
http://www.lazy-dog.demon.co.uk/wolves/
Wolverhampton Wanderers (Official)
http://www.idiscover.co.uk/wolves/

ENGLISH DIVISION 2

AFC Bournemouth
http://www.bath.ac.uk/~ee6dlah/club.htm
AFC Bournemouth
http://www.homeusers.prestel.co.uk/rose220/afcb1.htm
AFC Bournemouth
http://www.maths.soton.ac.uk/rpb/AFCB.html
AFC Bournemouth
http://www.maths.soton.ac.uk/rpb/AFCB.html
AFC Bournemouth
http://www.geocities.com/TimesSquare/Arcade/7499/afcb.htm
AFC Bournemouth (Official)
http://www.afcb.co.uk/
Blackpool
http://web.ukonline.co.uk/Members/c.moffat/basil/
Bristol City
http://ourworld.compuserve.com/homepages/redrobins/
Bristol Rovers
http://dialspace.dial.pipex.com/town/street/xko88/
Bristol Rovers
http://members.wbs.net/homepages/l/a/r/lardon/
Bristol Rovers
http://www.cf.ac.uk/uwcc/engin/brittonr/rovers/index.html
Bristol Rovers
http://www.geocities.com/Colosseum/6542/
Bristol Rovers
http://www.personal.unet.com/~coley/rovers/
Bristol Rovers
http://www.btinternet.com/~uk/BRFC/
Bristol Rovers
http://www.btinternet.com/~uk/BristolRovers/index.html
Bristol Rovers
http://www.cowan.edu.au/~gprewett/gas.htm
Bristol Rovers
http://www.cf.ac.uk/uwcc/engin/brittonr/rovers/index.html
Burnley
http://www.zensys.co.uk/home/page/trevor.ent/
Burnley
http://www.theturf.demon.co.uk/burnley.htm
Burnley
http://www.zen.co.uk/home/page/p.bassek/
Burnley
http://www.mtattersall.demon.co.uk/index.html
Burnley
http://home.sol.no/~parald/burnley/
Burnley
http://www.geocities.com/Colosseum/7075/index.html
Carlisle United
http://www.aston.ac.uk/~jonespm/
Carlisle United
http://dspace.dial.pipex.com/town/square/ad969/
Chester City [Silly Sausage - good history]
http://www.sillysausage.demon.co.uk/history.htm
Chester City (Official)
http://www.chester-city.co.uk/
Gillingham
http://ourworld.compuserve.com/homepages/gillsf.c/
Grimsby Town
http://www.aston.ac.uk/~etherina/index.html
Preston North End [unofficial - PNEWeb HomePage]
http://freespace.virgin.net/paul.billington/PNEWeb_homepage.html
Preston North End [unofficial - PNE Pages]
http://www.dpne.demon.co.uk/pages/pagesf.html
Preston North End [pie muncher online - front door]
http://www.pylonvu.demon.co.uk/pm/pm.html

Swansea City
http://www2.prestel.co.uk/gmartin/index.html
Wrexham
http://www.aber.ac.uk/~deg/wxm/text.html
Wrexham
http://www.csm.uwe.ac.uk/~klhender/wxm/index.html
Wycombe Wanderers
http://ourworld.compuserve.com/homepages/chairboys/

ENGLISH DIVISION 3

Brighton and Hove Albion
http://www.bmharding.demon.co.uk/seagulls/index.html/
Brighton and Hove Albion
http://homepages.enterprise.net/gjc/
Brighton and Hove Albion
http://www.aber.ac.uk/~bmh1/seagulls/
Cardiff City (Official)
http://www.styrotech.co.uk/ccafc/
Cardiff City
http://www.cf.ac.uk/uwcm/mg/bloo/biz.html
Cardiff City
http://www.geocities.com/Colosseum/1943/
Cardiff City
http://ds.dial.pipex.com/m4morris/ccafc.htm
Chester City
http://www.sillysausage.demon.co.uk/others.htm
Halifax Town
http://www.geocities.com/Colosseum/Stadium/3043/
Halifax Town [Aussie Style]
http://expage.com/page/Shaymen
Halifax Town [Shaymen]
http://www.shaymen.clara.net/shaymen.html
Hull City
http://www.demon.co.uk/Vox/hullcity/hullcity.html
Hull City
http://www.hullcity.demon.co.uk/
Leyton Orient (Official -OriNet)
http://www.matchroom.com/orient/
Leyton Orient [WebOrient - Global Orient Website]
http://www.web-orient.clara.net/
Macclesfield Town
http://www.cs.man.ac.uk/~griffitm/macctown/
Mansfield Town
http://www.footballnews.co.uk/clubs/1068/home.htm
Notts County
http://home.sol.no/~benn/magpienet/
Notts County
http://www.nbs.ntu.ac.uk/Staff/baylidj/ncfc.htm
Notts County
http://www.nbs.ntu.ac.uk/Staff/baylidj/ncfc.htm
Notts County
http://www.athene.net/soccercity/europe/eng/nc.htm
Notts County
http://www.imsport.co.uk/imsport/ims/tt/032/032.html
Scunthorpe United [The Iron Network]
http://www.fortunecity.com/wembley/villa/56/index.html
Scunthorpe United [Mailing List]
http://www.isfa.com/isfa/lists/scunthorpe/
Scunthorpe United [Iron World]
http://freespace.virgin.net/su.fc/
Shrewsbury Town
http://www.netlink.co.uk/users/ian/shrews/shrews.html
Shrewsbury Town
http://www.shrewsburytown.co.uk/
Swansea City
http://homepages.enterprise.net/gmartin/
Swansea City
http://homepages.enterprise.net/gmartin/indexnf.html

SCOTTISH PREMIER LEAGUE

Aberdeen - Official
http://www.afc.co.uk/site/
Aberdeen
http://homepages.enterprise.net/howburn/
Aberdeen
http://www.web13.co.uk/dons/
Aberdeen
http://www.raik.grid9.net/dons/
Aberdeen
http://www.raik.demon.co.uk/dons/
Aberdeen
http://freespace.virgin.net/a.morrison/ajm/afchome2.htm
Celtic (Official)
http://www.celticfc.co.uk/presecurity2.html
Celtic
http://www.erols.com/gbrown/dccelts.htm
Celtic
http://www.presence.co.uk/soccer/pages/history.html
Dundee United
http://www.algonet.se/~snoe/dfc/
Dundee United
http://www.arabland.demon.co.uk/news.htm
Dunfermline Athletic
http://www.webadvertising.co.uk/wwwboard/pars2/
Dunfermline Athletic [Soccernet]
http://www.soccernet.com/scottish/dafc/index.html
Dunfermline Athletic
http://www.aiai.ed.ac.uk/~wth/dunfermline/dunfermline.html
Heart of Midlothian (Official)
http://www.heartsfc.co.uk/
Heart of Midlothian [No Idle Talk - okay]
http://web.ukonline.co.uk/Members/grant.thorburn/nit1.htm
Heart of Midlothian
http://jambos.aurdev.com/update.html
Heart of Midlothian [has a squad list. USA]
http://www.geocities.com/Colosseum/Arena/2659/
Heart of Midlothian [Electronic Jam Tart]
http://www.ednet.co.uk/~ricw/
Heart of Midlothian [M'chester Hearts fans]
http://www.rigor.demon.co.uk/manheart.htm
Heart of Midlothian [OrwellHeartsSC]
http://members.aol.com/orwellhsc/orwellhearts/index.html
Heart of Midlothian [Midlands Hearts]
http://members.aol.com/gsha27/midlandhearts1.htm
Heart of Midlothian [Hearts Supporters USA - not very informative]
http://jambos.aurdev.com/
Heart of Midlothian [Always The Bridesmaid]
http://ourworld.compuserve.com/homepages/a_macdougall_and_ATB/
Heart of Midlothian [Rainbow Hearts S.C. Homepage]
http://ourworld.compuserve.com/homepages/andy_rainbow_hearts/
Kilmarnock
http://homepages.enterprise.net/wallace/
Kilmarnock
http://www.enterprise.net/kilmarnockfc/index.htm
Motherwell
http://www.isfa.com/server/web/motherwell/
Rangers (Official) [you need to register]
http://www.rangers.co.uk/channels/
Rangers
http://www.ukfootballpages.com/rangers/
Rangers
http://www.cee.hw.ac.uk/~johnc/Rangers/homepage.html
Rangers
http://www.geocities.com/Tokyo/Flats/5554/home.html
Rangers
http://www.geocities.com/Colosseum/Field/2968/
Rangers
http://dspace.dial.pipex.com/x-static/rangers.htm
Rangers
http://www.sgwoozy.force9.co.uk/rangers.html
Rangers
http://www.geocities.com/Colosseum/Track/7990/
Rangers
http://members.aol.com/broxinet/index.html

WEBSITE NOTES

WIN A FREE FOOTBALL BOOK!

Thank-you for buying a copy of our soccer yearbooks, covering all teams in the English Premiership, Scottish Premiership, and English Divisions 1, 2 and 3. We hope that you are happy with your purchase.

This unique collection of yearbooks, gives each supporter in the land their own club diary, supported by all-action shots from the greatest highlights of the last season, plus a diary from July 1998 – June 1999, detailing all club fixtures for the season.

If you would like to be kept informed of other football titles and next season's yearbooks, please cut out and complete this form and mail it back to me: Sharon Pitcher – Marketing Manager, Parragon, 13 Whiteladies Road, Bristol, BS8 1PB. Ten Lucky respondents will receive a free football book for their trouble!

Name of Favourite Team(s) ....
....

Name of Local Team(s) ....
....

Where did you buy this book? ....

Your Name: ....

Street: ....

Town: ....

County: ....

Postcode: ....

Email: ....

❏ Yes – please keep me informed of other football titles, plus next season's football yearbooks.

This information is being collected on behalf of Parragon Book Services Ltd.

For office use only